Steck Vaughn

Phonics

Level C

Reviewers

Terese D'Amico
Gifted Education Specialist for Grades 3–6
Thomas Jefferson Magnet School
Euclid, Ohio

Sandy Harrison
First Grade Teacher/Instructional Coordinator
Joe Wright Elementary School
Jacksonville, Texas

Dinah Costello
Third Grade Teacher/Assistant Principal
Holy Angels School
Colma, California

Dr. Marti O'Brien
Resource Specialist for Alternative Education
Polk County Schools
Bartow, Florida

Terry Redd
Second Grade Teacher
Don Shute Elementary School
East Peoria, Illinois

SBN 0-7398-9137-5

© 2004 Harcourt Achieve Inc.

All rights reserved. No part of the material protected by this copyright may be reproduced or utilized in any form or by any means, in whole or in part, without permission in writing from the copyright owner. Requests for permission should be mailed to: Copyright Permissions, Harcourt Achieve, P.O. Box 26015, Austin, Texas 78755.

Rigby and Steck-Vaughn are trademarks of Harcourt Achieve Inc. registered in the United States of America and/or other jurisdictions.

2 3 4 5 6 7 8 030 11 10 09 08 07 06 05

www.HarcourtAchieve.com
1.800.531.5015

Acknowledgments

Grateful acknowledgment is made to the following authors and publishers for permission to use copyrighted materials. Every effort has been made to trace ownership of all copyrighted material and to secure the necessary permissions to reprint. We express regret in advance for any error or omission. Any oversight will be acknowledged in future printings.

"Dream." Reprinted with the permission of the publisher, Children's Book Press, San Francisco, CA. From the book "Laughing Tomatoes and Other Spring Poems." Poem copyright © 1997 by Francisco X. Alarcón.

"Jim." Copyright © 1956 BY GWENDOLYN BROOKS BLAKELY. Used by permission of HarperCollins Publishers.

"Lunch Time." Copyright © 1996 by Lee Bennet Hopkins. Reprinted by permission of Curtis Brown, Ltd.

"Mice" from *Fifty-one New Nursery Rhymes* by Rose Fyleman. Copyright 1931, 1932 by Doubleday, a division of Bantam Doubleday Dell Publishing Group, Inc. Used by permission of Doubleday, a division of Bantam Doubleday Dell Publishing Group, Inc., and The Society of Authors as the Literary Representative of the Estate of Rose Fyleman.

"Pancake Collector." TEXT COPYRIGHT © 1978 BY JACK PRELUTSKY. Used by permission of HarperCollins Publishers.

"Pick Up Your Room" from *Fathers, Mothers, Sisters, Brothers* by Mary Ann Hoberman; illustrated by Marilyn Hafner. Copyright 1991 by Mary Ann Hoberman; illustrations copyright 1991 by Marilyn Hafner. By permission Little, Brown and Company.

"Puzzled" by Margaret Hillert. Used by permission of the author who controls all rights.

Photography by Digital Studios, Austin, Texas and Park Street Photography with the exceptions listed below.

The stock agencies have been abbreviated as follows:

AA: Animals Animals; C: Corbis; GH: Grant Heilman Photography, Inc.; IW: The Image Works; PE: PhotoEdit; PR: Photo Researchers; SB: Stock Boston; SM: The Stock Market; SS: Superstock; TI: Tony Stone International; UN: Uniphoto; US: Unicorn Stock Photos.

(ambulance) © Barry Runk/GH; (ant) Runk/Schoenberger/GH; (baby) © SS; (band) © Mary Kate Denny/PE; (beagle) © Ralph Reinhold/AA; (beak) © Arthur Smith III/GH; (bear) © Runk/Schoenberger/GH; (beard) © Brenda Tharp/PR; (bee) © Stephen Dalton/AA; (beetle) © Nigel Cattlin/PR; (beg) © Tim Davis/PR; (boat) © Bachmann/PR; (boxer) © SS; (bride) © Michael A. Keller/SM; (bridge) © UN; (bug) © Roy Morsh/SM; (cabin) © TI; (calves) © Renee Lynn/PR; (chandelier) © SS; (chauffeur) © Pete Saloutos/SM; (cheek) © SS; (cheer) © Myrleen Ferguson/PE; (chew) © SS; (chef) © Doug Martin/PR; (chemicals) © Rosenfeld Images/PR; (chemist) © Dennis O'Clair/TI; (chick) © Tim Davis/TI; (child) © Jon Feingersh/SM; (chin) © Eric Berndt/US; (chorus) © Myrleen Ferguson/PE; (city) © Superstock; (cloud) © Craig Tuttle/SM; (clouds) © Tony Craddock/TI; (colt) © Larry Lefever/GH; (cow) © Gi Bernard/AA; (couple) © SS; (crab) © Bruce Forster/TI; (crawl) © Myrleen Ferguson/PE; (crow) © Peter Saloutous/SM; (cry) © Tom McCarthy/PR; (cub) © PhotoDisc; (dad) © Jon Feingersh/SM; (dam) Tennessee Valley Authority; (deer) © PhotoDisc; (dolphin) © F. Stuart Westmoreland/PR; (dome) © Superstock; (drink) © UN; (duck) © Robert Maier/AA; (dune) © SS; (elephant) © James Balog/TI; (fight) © David Young-Wolff/PE; (fireplace) © Tony Freeman/PE; (fish) © Fred McConnaughey/PR; (fly) © Donald Specker/AA; (frog) © Tom Brakefield/SM; (gate) © Robert W. Ginn/US; (gerbil) © Robert Maier/AA; (goat) © James Marshall/SM; (gold) © T. Tracey/FPG; (haul) © Jr. Williams/Earth Scenes; (hawk) © PhotoDisc; (hay) © Tony Craddock/TI; (herd) ©SS; (hike) © Bill Beatty/Earth Scenes; (horse) © SS; (hut) Margo Moss/US; (jay) © Michael Bisceglie/AA; (jog) © Bruno Maso/PR; (juggle) © Richard Hutchings/PR; (jump) © David Young-Wolff/PE; (kitchen) © Willie Hill/FPG; (knight) © Claudia Kunin/TI; (lake) © Scott Melcer; (lamb) © Henry Auloos/AA; (lawn) © Bruce Forster/TI; (leash) © Mary Kate Denny/PE; (lion) © PhotoDisc; (lip) © David Young Wolff/PE; (lizard) © PhotoDisc; (man) © SS; (mare) © Robert Maier/AA; (meet) © Michael Newman/PE; (mice) © Roger Jackman/AA; (mole) © Charles Mohr/PR; (mouse) © J. M. Labat/Jacana/PR; (mouth) © Michael Newman/PE; (mow) © David Frazier/PR; (mule) © Karen Holsinger Mullen/US; (nap) © SS; (noise) © Michael Newman/PE; (nose) © UN; (nurse) ATC Productions/SM; (orchestra) © Tony Freeman/PE; (orchid) © Charles Marden Fitch/SS; (owl) © PhotoDisc; (parachute) © SS; (parrot) © PhotoDisc; (point) © Michael Newman/PE; (porch) © Jim Shippee/US; (post) © Michael Habicht/Earth Scenes; (prize) © PhotoDisc; (puppies) © SS; (pyramid) © Adam G. Sylvester/PR; (queen) © Hulton-Deutsch/C; (rabbit, raccoon) © PhotoDisc; (reach) © Laura Dwight/C; (rein) © SS; (robin) © Alan G. Nelson/AA; (roof) © Larry Lefever/GH; (run) © Rich Baker/US; (sad) © Kevin Cavanagh/PR; (sail) © Jim Brown/SM; (scream) © Chris Collins/SM; (seal) © Patti Murray/AA; (seed) © SS; (shark) © W. Gregory Brown/AA; (sheep) © Tim Davis/PR; (skunk) © PhotoDisc; (sky) © Michael Busselle/TI; (sleep) © Myrleen Ferguson/PE; (sleigh) © Guy Gillette/PR; (slide) © Michael Newman/PE; (smile) © SS; (smoke) © Barry Rowland/TI; (snake) © PhotoDisc; (snail) © Peter Steiner/SM; (snow) © Craig Tuttle/SM; (snowflake) © Gerben Oppermans/TI; (splash) © Ray Massey/TI; (squirrel) © Laurie Campbell/TI; (strong) © Gerard Vandystadt/PR; (swim) © Kathy Ferguson/PE; (team) © Kaufmann/SM; (them) © Rob Lewine/SM; (tiger) © PhotoDisc; (toad) © Kevin & Sue Hanley/AA; (tree) © Rich Iwasaki/TI; (trophy) © PhotoDisc; (turkeys) © Robert Maier/AA; (use) © Bill Aaron/PE; (vault) © SS; (vet) © Dimaggio/Kalish/SM; (volcano) © SS; (wall) © Leslie Borden/PE; (walrus) © SS; (wasp) © Stephen Dalton/AA; (wave) © Warren Bolster/TI; (weed) © Gabe Palmer/SM; (weigh) © David Young-Wolff/PE; (whale) © Gerald Lim/US; (wheat) © Kevin R. Morris/TI; (yawn) © Aneal Vohra/US; (zebra) © PhotoDisc.

Additional Photography: p. 5 © Tom McHugh/Photo Researchers (mouse); © PhotoDisc Inc. (popsicles); p. 8 © Corel Corp.; p. 19 © Robert Maier/Animals Animals; p. 23 © Ed Elberfeld/Uniphoto (girl); p. 39 © Japack/Corbis Westlight; p. 65 © Nicholas Russell/The Image Bank; © Myrleen Ferguson/PhotoEdit (balloon); p. 82 © Tom Prettyman/PhotoEdit; p. 86 © Jeff Greenberg/Photo Researchers; p. 91 © Lawrence Migdale/Photo Researchers (boy eating); © Image Club Graphics, Inc. (Eiffel Tower); © PhotoDisc Inc. (maracas); p. 96 © Superstock, Inc. (apartments, farm); p. 97 © Allan Friedlander/Superstock (Irish house); © Paul Harris/Tony Stone Images (Irish lake); p. 98 © PhotoDisc Inc. (green beans, root vegetables); © MetaTools, Inc. (corn); p. 100 © Doug Armand/Tony Stone Images (pyramids-top); © Sylvain Grandadam/Tony Stone Images (pyramids-bottom); p. 103 © Nigel Hicks/Superstock; p. 106 © Connie Coleman/Tony Stone Images; p. 112 © PhotoDisc Inc. (eagle); © Corel Corp. (rocket); © Image Club Graphics, Inc. (Eiffel Tower); © MetaTools, Inc. (ant, beetle); p. 119 © Joel Rogers/Tony Stone Images (pond); © Bruce Forster/Tony Stone Images (fish); p. 120 © David G. Houser/Corbis Media (parrot); © Alan D. Carey/Photo Researchers (iguana); © David R. Frazier/Photo Researchers (snake); p. 123 © Myrleen Ferguson/PhotoEdit (mom & son); p. 125 © COMSTOCK; p. 139 © Nancy Brown/The Image Bank; p. 148 © Tom Rosenthal/Superstock (boy); © COMSTOCK (girl); p. 149 © Scott Barrow, Inc./Superstock (flowers); © Fotografia/Corbis Westlight (recycling); p. 156 © Anthony Botera/Superstock; p. 161 © Robert Llewellyn/Superstock (ambulance); © Tom Rosenthal/Superstock (coach); p. 165 © D. Van Kirk/The Image Bank (pancakes); © Superstock, Inc. (coins); p. 167 © Richard T. Nowitz/Corbis Media; p. 168 © Peter Johnson/Corbis Media (rocks); © MetaTools, Inc. (magnifying glass); p. 169 © PhotoDisc Inc. (marbles, insect box); p. 170 © Superstock, Inc. (letters); © Koji Kitagawa/Superstock (stamps); p. 171 © David Northcott/Superstock; p. 174 © Superstock, Inc. (magnifying glass, coins); p. 178 © MetaTools, Inc. (butterflies 1-4); © PhotoDisc Inc. (butterfly 5); p. 179 © Koji Kitagawa/Superstock (shells); © David Spindel/Superstock (dolls); p. 183 © Image Color/Index Stock Imagery (girl); p. 195 © Tom Murphy/Superstock.

Additional royalty-free photography by Corbis Royalty Free, Photos.com Royalty Free, and PhotoDisc/Getty Royalty Free.

Level C Contents

Unit 1 — Consonants
Theme: My Favorite Things

Poem: "Mice" by Rose Fyleman 5
Family Involvement 6
Initial Consonants 7–8
Final Consonants 9–10
Medial Consonants 11–12
Sounds of *c, g,* and *s* 13–15
Reading Words with Hard and Soft *c* and *g* and Variant Sounds of *s* in Context 16
Spelling Words with Consonants 17
Consonants Review 18
Reading Words with Consonants in Context 19
Writing Words with Consonants 20
Check-up Unit 1 21–22

Unit 2 — Short and Long Vowels
Theme: I Wonder

Poem: "Puzzled" by Margaret Hillert 23
Family Involvement 24
Short Vowels 25–34
Short Vowels *a, o,* and *i* Review 35
Short Vowels *u* and *e* Review 36
Spelling Words with Short Vowels 37
Short Vowels Review 38
Reading Short Vowel Words in Context 39
Writing Short Vowel Words 40
Long Vowels *a, o,* and *i* 41–46
Exceptions for Vowels *o* and *i* 47–48
Long Vowels *a, o,* and *i* Review 49–50
Long Vowels *u* and *e* 51–54
Long Vowels *u* and *e* Review 55–56
Syllables 57–58
Spelling Words with Long Vowels 59
Long Vowels Review 60
Reading Long Vowel Words in Context 61
Writing Long Vowel Words 62
Check-up Unit 2 63–64

Unit 3 — Consonant Blends and Digraphs, Silent Consonants
Theme: A Dream Away

Poem: "Dream" by Francisco X. Alarcón 65
Family Involvement 66
Initial *s, r, l,* and *tw* Blends 67–72
Final Blends 73–74
Initial and Final Blends Review 75–76
Consonant Digraphs *ch, sh, th, wh, ph,* and *gh* .. 77–80
Final Consonant Digraphs *ch, sh, th, ck, ng, nk,* and *tch* 81
Initial, Medial, and Final Consonant Digraphs 82
Silent Consonants 83–84
Spelling Words with Consonant Blends and Digraphs and Silent Consonants 85
Consonant Blends and Digraphs and Silent Consonants Review 86
Reading Words with Consonant Blends and Digraphs and Silent Consonants in Context 87
Writing Words with Consonant Blends and Digraphs and Silent Consonants 88
Check-up Unit 3 89–90

Unit 4 — r-Controlled Vowels, y as a Vowel, Vowel Digraphs, Diphthongs
Theme: Around the World

Poem: "Lunch Time" by Lee Bennett Hopkins 91
Family Involvement 92
r-Controlled Vowels *ar, or, er, ir, ur, air, are, ear,* and *eer* 93–97
Syllables in Words with *r*-Controlled Vowels 98
y as a Vowel 99
Syllables in Words with *y* as a Vowel 100
Spelling Words with *r*-Controlled Vowels and *y* as a Vowel 101
r-Controlled Vowels and *y* as a Vowel Review 102
Reading Words with *r*-Controlled Vowels and *y* as a Vowel in Context 103
Writing Words with *r*-Controlled Vowels and *y* as a Vowel 104
Vowel Digraphs *ea, ei, oo, ew, ui, au, aw,* and *al* 105–112
ou as a Vowel Digraph 113
ou as a Diphthong 114
Sounds of *ow* 115
Diphthongs *oy* and *oi* 116

(continued)

Unit 4 (continued)

Spelling Words with Vowel Digraphs and Diphthongs............ 117
Vowel Digraphs and Diphthongs Review 118
Reading Words with Vowel Digraphs and Diphthongs in Context.............. 119
Writing Words with Vowel Digraphs and Diphthongs........................ 120
Check-up Unit 4 121–122

Unit 5 Compound Words, Schwa, Inflectional Endings, Syllables, Plurals, Contractions, Possessives

Theme: Helping Out

Poem: "Jim" by Gwendolyn Brooks 123
Family Involvement 124
Compound Words 125–126
Schwa 127–128
Inflectional Endings -s, -es, -ed, -ing, -er and -est........................... 129–130
Spelling Compounds, Words with Schwa, and Words with Inflectional Endings............. 131
Compounds, Schwa, and Inflectional Endings Review 132
Reading Compounds, Words with Schwa, and Words with Inflectional Endings in Context..... 133
Writing Compounds, Words with Schwa, and Words with Inflectional Endings........... 134
Syllables 135–150
Syllables Review 151–152
Plurals............................... 153–154
Contractions 155–156
Singular Possessives..................... 157
Plural Possessives 158
Spelling Plurals, Contractions, and Possessives 159
Plurals, Contractions, and Possessives Review 160
Reading Plurals, Contractions, and Possessives in Context 161
Writing Plurals, Contractions, and Possessives 162
Check-up Unit 5 163–164

Unit 6 Suffixes and Prefixes

Theme: Collector's Corner

Poem: from "The Pancake Collector" by Jack Prelutsky 165
Family Involvement 166
Suffixes -less, -ness, -y, -ful, -ly, -ment, -ion, -able, -en, -ous, -er, -or, and -ist 167–172
Prefixes un-, dis-, re-, -mis-, pre-, de-, im- and in-............................. 173–176
Spelling Words with Suffixes and Prefixes.... 177
Suffixes and Prefixes Review................... 178
Reading Words with Suffixes and Prefixes in Context 179
Writing Words with Suffixes and Prefixes..... 180
Check-up Unit 6 181–182

Unit 7 Dictionary Skills, Multiple-Meaning Words, Synonyms, Antonyms, Homonyms

Theme: At Home

Poem: "Pick Up Your Room" by Mary Ann Hoberman..................... 183
Family Involvement 184
Alphabetical Order..................... 185–186
Dictionary Guide Words 187–188
Locating Words in a Dictionary 189–190
Multiple-Meaning Words................ 191–192
Synonyms............................... 193
Antonyms............................... 194
Homonyms 195–196
Spelling Multiple-Meaning Words, Synonyms, Antonyms, and Homonyms................ 197
Dictionary Skills, Multiple-Meaning Words, Synonyms, Antonyms, and Homonyms Review 198
Reading Multiple-Meaning Words, Synonyms, Antonyms, and Homonyms in Context........ 199
Writing Synonyms, Antonyms, and Homonyms 200
Check-up Unit 7 201–202

Final Assessment 203–208
Definitions and Rules .... Inside Back Cover

UNIT 1
My Favorite Things
Consonants

Mice

I think mice
Are rather nice.

    Their tails are long,
    Their faces small,
    They haven't any
    Chins at all.
    Their ears are pink,
    Their teeth are white,
    They run about
    The house at night.
    They nibble things
    They shouldn't touch
    And no one seems
    To like them much.

But I think mice
Are nice.

Rose Fyleman

Think About It

Why don't some people like mice?
How do you feel about mice?

Dear Family of _____,

Your child will be reviewing consonant sounds, including the hard and soft sounds of c, as in *cat* and *city*, and g, as in *go* and *gym*. Your child will be using these sounds to read about favorite things. Here are some activities you can do together.

- Play c and g tick-tack-toe with your child. Make a grid of nine squares and write c's and g's in the squares instead of x's and o's. A player must name a word that has the soft sound for his or her letter (c or g) before writing that letter in a square. Play again, using the hard sounds for c and g.
- Have your child write any four consonants in the left-hand column of the chart below. For each category ask your child to write a word that begins or ends with the consonant on the left.

Estimada familia de _____,

Su niño o niña repasará los sonidos de las consonantes en inglés, incluyendo los sonidos fuertes y suaves de la c, como en *cat* y *city* y de la g, como en *go* y *gym*. Él o ella usará estos sonidos en su lectura sobre cosas favoritas. Algunas actividades que usted y su niño o niña pueden hacer en inglés aparecen a continuación.

- Juntos jueguen a tres en raya con c y g. Hagan una gráfica de nueve cuadros y escriban las letras c y g en los cuadros en vez de x y o. Un jugador debe decir una palabra que tenga el sonido en suave de la c o g antes de escribir esa letra en un cuadro. Vuelvan a jugar usando esta vez los sonidos fuertes de la c y la g.
- Pídale a su niño o niña que escriba cuatro consonantes que quiera en la columna a la izquierda de la tabla que aparece arriba. Luego, pídale que escriba una palabra que empiece o termine con la consonante a la izquierda.

LIBRARY LINK

You might like to visit the library and find the book *Insects Are My Life* by Megan McDonald. Read it with your child.

	Foods	Animals	Colors

Unit 1: Family Involvement

Say each picture name. Write the consonant that stands for the first sound.

RULE The first sound in many words is a consonant sound.

Unit 1: Initial Consonants

Circle the word that completes each sentence. Write the word on the line.

1. I like to visit the _____. park lark bark

2. I went there last _____ with my friend. peak seek week

3. The park ranger rode in a _____. jeep leap weep

4. I saw a _____ on the side of a hill. door deer dare

5. Jana fed _____ to a squirrel. cuts quits nuts

6. The _____ would not come out of its shell. rattle turtle bottle

7. I saw a _____ with blue feathers. best bell bird

8. Jana saw a _____ with a yellow stripe. fish fur fry

9. A _____ robin hopped close to me. hung young gong

10. We were very _____ as we watched it. quiet kite diet

Choose a sentence. Ask your child to replace the missing word with a different word and to identify its beginning consonant.

Unit 1: Initial Consonants

Say each picture name. Write the consonant that stands for the **last** sound to complete the word.

RULE The **last** sound in many words is a **consonant** sound.

**Circle the word that completes each sentence.
Write the word on the line.**

1. I like to visit my dad at _____.	work	wood	worm
2. We drive the _____ to get there.	can	cat	car
3. The _____ is bumpy.	road	roam	roar
4. We listen to _____ on the radio.	moon	must	music
5. The workers _____ a big hole.	did	dim	dig
6. Dad wears a hard _____ on his head.	hat	has	ham
7. He keeps a _____ behind his ear.	pedal	pencil	pepper
8. I fill a _____ with rocks.	box	bog	boy
9. We sit on the _____ and eat our lunch.	grass	grab	grill
10. We watch the workers build a _____.	dam	dab	dad

10 Unit 1: Final Consonants

AT HOME Read the answer choices for three of the sentences. Ask your child to identify the final consonant in each word.

Unit 1: Medial Consonants

Help Alan make a list of his favorite foods. Write the words that name foods under the picture of the salad. Write the other words under the picture of the robot. Then write the consonant that stands for the middle sound in each word.

| bacon | butter | cabin | carrot | honey | kitten | lemon | lesson |
| medal | melon | motel | muffin | peanut | siren | spider | tulip |

Unit 1: Medial Consonants

Ask your child to choose three words from the list and identify the beginning consonant in each word.

cat   city

Read each sentence. Circle the words that contain the letter **c**. Then write the words with the **soft c** sound in the picture of the **city**. Write the words with the **hard c** sound in the picture of the **cat**.

RULE The letter **c** can stand for more than one sound. It can stand for the **hard c** sound you hear in **cat**. Hard **c** sounds like **k**. When **e, i,** or **y** comes after **c**, the **c** usually stands for the **soft c** sound you hear in **city**.

1. I like the city more than the country.
2. It is fun to live in the center of things.
3. It is nice to skate on ice in the park.
4. I can get a taxicab on a corner.
5. I like to see actors in a play.
6. I love living in a big place.

gas

giraffe

Gerry's favorite words contain the **soft g** sound. Gail's favorite words contain the **hard g** sound. Say each word in the box. Write Gerry's favorite words on his sign. Write Gail's favorite words on her sign.

RULE The letter **g** can stand for more than one sound. It can stand for the **hard g** sound you hear in **gas**. When **e, i,** or **y** comes after **g**, the **g** usually stands for the **soft g** sound you hear in **giraffe**. Soft **g** sounds like **j**.

flag	game	gate	gem	gentle	gerbil	germ
giant	ginger	gold	good	guitar	gym	huge
igloo	mug	page	pigeon	sugar	tiger	

Gerry

Gail

14 Unit 1: Hard and Soft *g*

AT HOME — Ask your child to use each of the words from the box in a sentence.

sock   rose   sugar   tissue

Say each picture name. Write the sound the **s** stands for—**s, z,** or **sh**—on the line. Then circle the word or words in each sentence that have that sound of **s**.

RULE The letter **s** can stand for more than one sound. It can stand for the **s** sound you hear in **sock** and the **z** sound you hear in **rose**. The letter **s** and the letters **ss** can also stand for the **sh** sound you hear in **sugar** and **tissue**.

1. Keep a tissue in your pocket.

_____ 2. Make sure you come home on time.

3. Mom will serve me soup and salad.

_____ 4. Sandy is too sick to go outside.

5. Use your nose to find the rose.

_____ 6. She likes peas and beans and french fries.

Find the word in the box that completes each sentence. Write the word on the line.

7. Sam knows how to make his favorite _____.

8. He puts _____ on some bread.

9. His mom grills the food and serves it for _____.

10. Sam is _____ that his mom is the best cook.

11. Sam smiles when he _____ her good food.

cheese
sandwich
smells
supper
sure

Name _____

Unit 1: Variant Sounds of **s**   15

Circle the words in each sentence that have **c** or **g**. Then write each word in the correct column.

1. I like to curl up with my favorite books.
2. One is about a big cat that skates on ice.
3. Another one is about a gentle giant who plays golf.
4. I am certain that I will always love to read.

hard c	soft c	hard g	soft g
_____	_____	_____	_____
_____	_____	_____	_____

Circle the words in each sentence that have **s**. Then write each word in the correct column.

5. Dan assured me that he has favorite books, too.
6. He read the one about a space mission.
7. He used a tissue when he read about the sad prince.
8. We both like the book about country music.

s sound of s	z sound of s	sh sound of s
_____	_____	_____
_____	_____	_____
_____	_____	_____

Unit 1: Reading Words with Hard and Soft *c* and *g* and Variant Sounds of *s* in Context

Have your child look in books for words that have hard and soft *c* and *g* sounds, as well as words with the *s, z,* and *sh* sounds of *s*.

Say each picture name. Write the word on the line.

candle
cent
cheese
gem
gold
sugar

1.  _____
2.  _____
3.  _____
4.  _____
5.  _____
6.  _____

Find the word in the box that matches each clue. Write the word in the puzzle.

camel   car   city   hose   leaves
paper   present   seven   tissue   tulip

Across
2. a kind of flower
6. an animal with a hump on its back
7. 3 + 4
8. an automobile
9. a gift

Down
1. thin, soft paper
3. used to spray water
4. used to write on
5. what falls off a tree in autumn
8. a large town

Name _____

Unit 1: Spelling Words with Consonants

17

Each word in the box is in the puzzle. Find and circle each word. Words go across and down.

busy	cat
cider	cover
giraffe	good
gym	inside
leaf	mug
nice	nose
pot	sack
sure	tissue

```
g  i  r  a  f  f  e  c  a  t
z  s  a  c  k  g  w  y  m  i
t  n  f  a  d  o  o  d  l  s
e  o  c  l  g  o  g  y  m  s
w  s  i  b  u  d  m  u  g  u
n  u  d  c  i  n  s  i  d  e
n  r  e  c  o  v  e  r  s  p
i  e  r  w  d  y  v  t  u  o
c  i  t  i  a  b  u  s  y  t
e  l  e  a  f  x  n  o  s  e
```

Find the word in the box that completes each sentence. Write the word on the line.

bus	grill
lessons	peanut
walrus	zebra

1. I like to ride the _____ to the zoo.

2. I learn many _____ about nature there.

3. The striped _____ is from Africa.

4. The _____ lives in the ocean and has big tusks.

5. There is a picnic area with a _____.

6. Dad cooks hot dogs, but I like my _____ butter sandwich better.

Unit 1: Consonants Review

Ask your child to make a list of zoo animals. Have your child point out the beginning, middle, and ending consonants in each word.

Read the passage. Then read the sentences below it. Write the word that completes each sentence.

Mice or Gerbils?

Carrie went to the pet shop. She couldn't decide whether to buy gerbils or mice. Carrie got books on mice and books on gerbils. This is what she learned about them.

Both gerbils and mice are rodents. All rodents have two long curved teeth in their top jaw.

Mice and gerbils are born blind and without fur. Their eyes open soon. They grow a coat of soft fur, too. Gerbils are fully grown when they are about 12 weeks old. Mice are grown at about 6 weeks.

A mouse's tail is longer than the rest of its body. Most of the tail is bare. A long, bare tail can help keep the animal cool. Mice that live in hot places have longer tails than mice that live in cool places. A gerbil's furry tail is as long as its body. It uses its tail for balance when it jumps.

Mice hide and sleep during the day and come out when it is dark. Gerbils rest during the hottest part of the day, too. They are also active at night.

1. Gerbils and mice are both _____.

2. A _____ uses its tail when it jumps.

3. Mice sleep during the _____.

4. Both gerbils and mice are _____ at night.

5. A long, bare tail helps keep a mouse _____.

Name _____

Unit 1: Reading Words with Consonants in Context

19

What is your favorite pet? Write a paragraph telling what your favorite pet is and why you like it. The words in the box may help you.

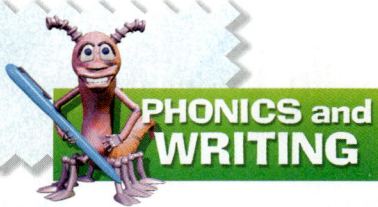

cage	cat	chews	dog	food
gerbil	hops	mouse	parrot	plays
rabbit	sleeps	toys	water	yellow

Unit 1: Writing Words with Consonants

Ask your child to read the paragraph to you.

Say each picture. Write the missing consonant to complete the word.

Unit 1 CHECK-UP

1. bo__er
2. __ate
3. ha__
4. __ugar
5. __i__e
6. __li__
7. __ym
8. ca__in
9. __eet
10. __up
11. __ock
12. ro__e
13. hu__
14. __em
15. mi__e
16. __oat
17. le__on
18. ha__
19. no__e
20. __ent

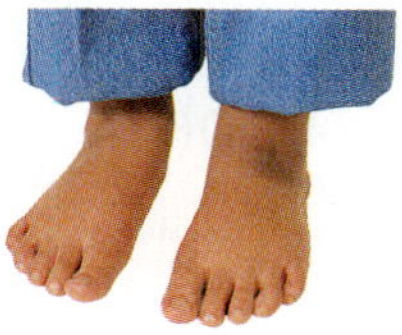

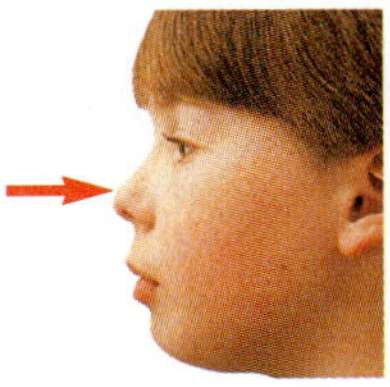

Name _____

Unit 1: Assessing Consonants — 21

Unit 1 CHECK-UP

Fill in the circle next to the word that completes each sentence.

1. I like _____ on a hot muffin.
   ○ buffer   ○ bumper   ○ butter   ○ bullet

2. Susan wears _____ ribbons in her hair.
   ○ gold   ○ cold   ○ sold   ○ hold

3. I am _____ that Latin music is my favorite.
   ○ cure   ○ lure   ○ sure   ○ pure

4. All my friends are _____.
   ○ nest   ○ nice   ○ Nile   ○ nip

5. I like to read _____ about sports.
   ○ cooks   ○ nooks   ○ hooks   ○ books

6. My mom likes a _____ of hot tea on a cold morning.
   ○ mug   ○ mutt   ○ mud   ○ muff

7. My dad likes to get up early to watch the sun _____.
   ○ rice   ○ ride   ○ ripe   ○ rise

8. Tom likes to read the front _____ of the newspaper.
   ○ pale   ○ page   ○ pace   ○ pane

9. Gerry and I like to sit on a _____ and look at the city.
   ○ hill   ○ him   ○ hid   ○ hip

10. We like to spend the night in a _____ in the woods.
    ○ camel   ○ cabin   ○ candle   ○ carrot

UNIT 2
I Wonder
Short and Long Vowels

Puzzled

I took a sip of lemon pop
And then a sip of lime,
A little orange soda, too,
A swallow at a time.
Some grape came next and cherry red.
And then I almost cried.
How *could* my stomach feel so bad
With rainbows down inside?

Margaret Hillert

Think About It

What does the speaker mean by "rainbows down inside"?
Why does the speaker's stomach feel bad?

Dear Family of _____,

Your child will be reviewing short and long vowels. Your child will be using these skills to read about the theme I Wonder. Here are some activities you can do together.

- Make a list of some words with short vowels and long vowels, such as *cat* and *rake*. Take turns making up and solving riddles about the words. In each riddle tell the vowel sound and the number of syllables in the word.
- Name a vowel sound, such as short *a* or long *o*. See how many words your child can write with that vowel sound in one minute.
- Invite your child to help you make a grocery list. Have your child point out any short vowel words and any long vowel words.

LIBRARY LINK

You might like to visit the library and find the book *Why Do Seasons Change?* from Dorling Kindersley's Why series. Read it with your child.

Estimada familia de _____,

Su niño o niña repasará los sonidos en inglés de las vocales llamadas "largas" y "cortas". Él o ella usará estos conocimientos en su lectura sobre el tema Me pregunto (I Wonder). Algunas actividades que usted y su niño o niña pueden hacer en inglés aparecen a continuación.

- Juntos hagan una lista de algunas palabras con vocales "largas" y "cortas", tales como *cat* y *rake*. Por turnos, inventen y resuelvan adivinanzas sobre estas palabras. Para cada adivinanza digan la vocal y el número de sílabas que contiene cada palabra.
- Nombre una vocal, tal como la "*a* corta" o la "*o* larga". Vea cuántas palabras con esa vocal puede escribir en un minuto su niño o niña.
- Invite a su niño o niña a que le ayude a escribir una lista de víveres. Pídale su niño o niña a indicar algunas palabras que tienen el sonido de vocales "largas" y algunas palabras que tienen el sonido de vocales "cortas".

 map

Say each picture name. If the word has the **short a** sound, write **a** to complete the word.

RULE If a word has only one vowel, the vowel sound is usually short. **Short a** is the vowel sound you hear in **map**.

1. b a g
2. d a d
3. p _ n
4. c a t
5. v e t
6. p a n
7. d a m
8. f a n
9. s a d
10. g a s
11. c a n
12. m o p
13. m a n
14. g u m
15. h a m
16. b a t

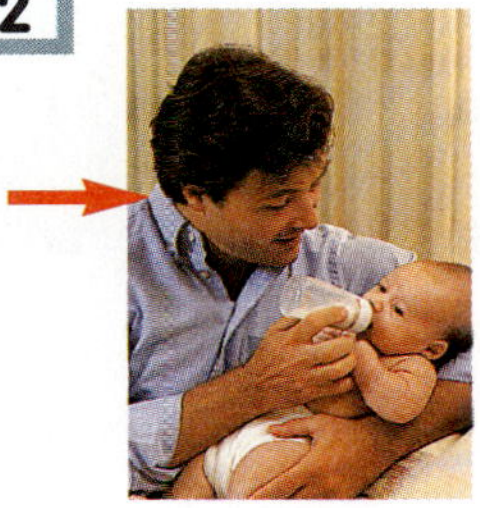

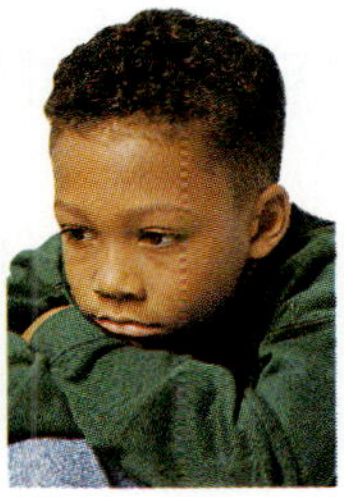

Name _____

Unit 2: Short Vowel *a* 25

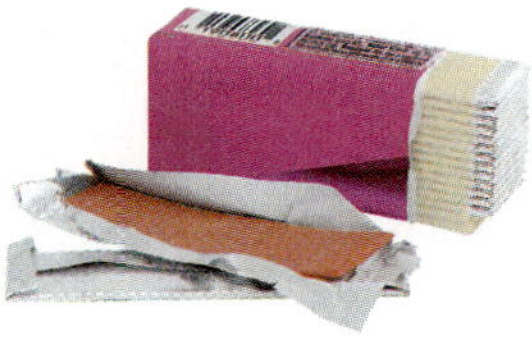

Circle the word that completes each sentence. Then write the word on the line.

1. Jan and her dad will _____ in the winter.   camp   cone
2. They _____ warm blankets.   pad   pack
3. Dad puts food in a big _____.   bag   bug
4. Then they load the _____.   van   vat
5. Dad stops to get some _____.   gas   gag
6. He looks at his _____, too.   mop   map
7. Dad drives _____ drives all day.   end   and
8. They _____ by towns and farms.   pass   pat
9. Winter _____ come to the woods.   has   his
10. Jan wonders where the _____ bears are.   block   black
11. Why don't they see the _____ squirrels?   fat   pat
12. Dad says these animals are _____ asleep.   fast   sat
13. They _____ sleep for a long time.   can   cap
14. Finally Jan and her dad are _____ the cabin.   it   at
15. At _____ they can sleep, too.   last   lost

Unit 2: Short Vowel *a*

Ask your child to use words on this page to tell you what happens when Jan and her dad wake up.

fox

Circle the word that names each picture. Then write the word on the line.

RULE If a word has only one vowel, the vowel sound is usually short. **Short o** is the vowel sound you hear in **fox**.

1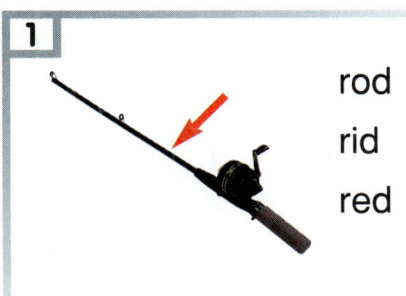
rod
rid
red
_____

2
jig
jog
jug
_____

3
cat
cut
cot
_____

4
log
lost
lock
_____

5
pit
pot
pat
_____

6
dog
dot
doll
_____

7
cot
cob
cod
_____

8
top
tip
tap
_____

9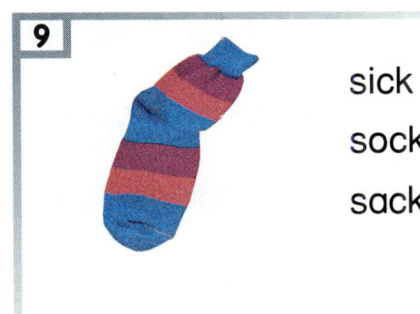
sick
sock
sack
_____

Draw lines to connect the rhyming words in each box.

10
fox   mop
hop   lock
dock   pod
nod   box

11
dot   hog
fog   song
cob   job
long   got

12
boss   stop
clock   lot
not   rock
pop   moss

Name _____

Unit 2: Short Vowel *o*   27

People have often made up stories to explain why things happen. Read each story title. Underline the word that has the **short o** sound. Write the word on the line.

1. Why the Rabbit Likes to Hop   _____
2. Why Dogs and Cats Fight   _____
3. Why the Sun Is So Hot   _____
4. Why Peas Have Pods   _____
5. Why the Ox Pulls Heavy Loads   _____
6. Why the Leopard Has Spots   _____
7. Why Ants Crawl on Logs   _____
8. Why the Fox Has a Bushy Tail   _____
9. Why Fish Live in Ponds   _____
10. Why Water Does Not Burn   _____
11. Why Hogs Like Mud   _____
12. Why Tadpoles Turn into Frogs   _____
13. Why Clocks Have Hands   _____
14. Why Birds Sing Songs   _____
15. Why Snakes Hide Under Rocks   _____

Unit 2: Short Vowel *o*

AT HOME Help your child make up two titles that include **short o** words to add to the list.

fish

Say each picture name. Write the word on the line.

RULE If a word has only one vowel, the vowel sound is usually short. **Short i** is the vowel sound you hear in **fish**.

1.  _____
2.  _____
3.  _____
4.  _____
5.  _____
6.  _____
7.  _____
8.  _____
9.  _____

Each word in the box is in the puzzle. Find and circle each word. The words go across, down, and at a slant.

d	i	d	o	m	d	a
w	l	i	t	b	i	g
o	i	m	i	s	s	w
j	z	t	d	u	h	e
r	h	b	h	i	l	l

big	did	dim	dish
hill	lit	miss	with

Name _____

Unit 2: Short Vowel *i*

Read the poem. Underline the words that have the **short i** sound. Then write the words on the lines below.

Have You Ever Wondered . . .

What it's like to be a fish
And give your tail a little swish?
To swim with your fins and dive and dip
And through the water quickly zip?

Do you ever wish . . .
You could roll and flip?
Or chase a ship
In the misty sea?
Or see a shrimp slip by
And simply let him be?

1. _____ 2. _____ 3. _____ 4. _____
5. _____ 6. _____ 7. _____ 8. _____
9. _____ 10. _____ 11. _____ 12. _____
13. _____ 14. _____ 15. _____ 16. _____
17. _____ 18. _____ 19. _____ 20. _____

Ask your child to choose three **short i** words from the poem and use each in a sentence.

cup

Say each picture name. If the word has the **short u** sound, write **u** to complete the word.

RULE If a word has only one vowel, the vowel sound is usually short. **Short u** is the vowel sound you hear in **cup**.

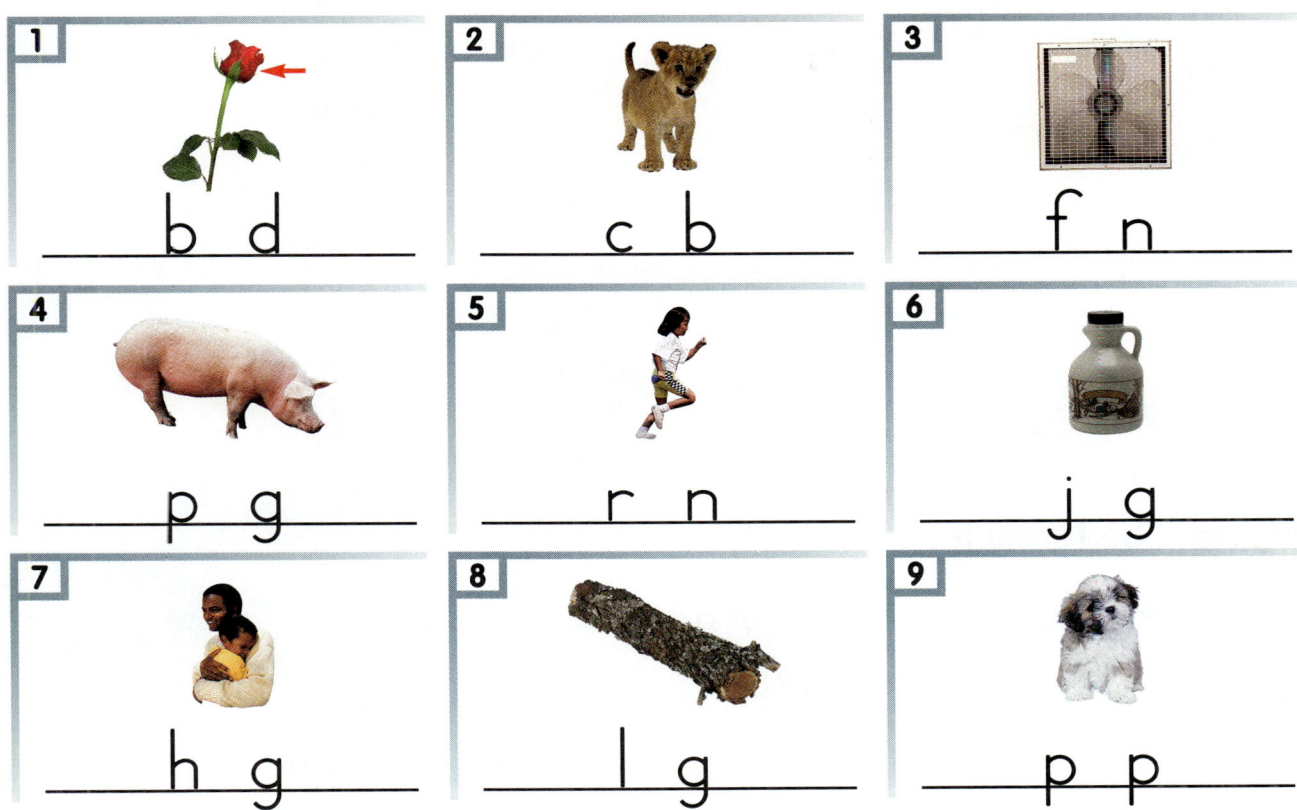

1. b __ d
2. c __ b
3. f __ n
4. p __ g
5. r __ n
6. j __ g
7. h __ g
8. l __ g
9. p __ p

Read each sentence. Find the word in dark print. Replace the vowel to make a **short u** word. Write the new word on the line.

10. I wonder how **big** a _____ can get.

11. I wonder how to make _____ out of **rags**.

12. We will need _____ to get this **lock** open.

13. I'll **dig** my hole deeper than the one you _____.

14. That squirrel will **not** be happy with just one _____.

15. It's lots of _____ to be a football **fan**.

Name _____

Unit 2: Short Vowel *u*   31

Find the word in the box that completes each question. Write the word on the line.

brush	bug	bus	buzz
cub	duck	run	skunk
stuck	sun	trunk	tub

Would it be funny if . . .

1. we rode in a balloon instead of a _____?

2. a _____ said "oink" instead of "quack"?

3. the _____ was blue and the sky was yellow?

4. your mother brought home a little bear _____?

5. you had to take a bath in a big wooden _____?

6. you had to use a comb to _____ your teeth?

7. an elephant had a nose instead of a _____?

8. all the bees refused to _____?

9. every _____ was as big as a car?

10. cats helped people who were _____ in trees?

11. a _____ was pink instead of black and white?

12. a snail could _____ as fast as a horse?

Unit 2: Short Vowel *u*

AT HOME

Ask your child to write a "Would it be funny if" question using a word with **short *u***.

bed

Circle the word that names each picture. Write the word on the line.

RULE If a word has only one vowel, the vowel sound is usually short. **Short e** is the vowel sound you hear in **bed**.

1.  vast / vest / vote
_____

2.  net / not / nut
_____

3. **10** tin / tan / ten
_____

4.  pig / pot / peg
_____

5.  bill / bell / bull
_____

6.  pen / pan / pin
_____

7.  red / rod / rid
_____

8.  big / bag / beg
_____

9.  cheek / chess / chain
_____

Say each picture name. If the word has the **short e** sound, write the word on the line.

10.
_____

11.
_____

12.
_____

13.
_____

14.
_____

15.
_____

16.
_____

17.
_____

Name _____

Unit 2: Short Vowel *e*

Read each group of sentences. Complete each sentence with a word at the right. Write the word on the line.

1. Do you know how to care for a _____?   set

   Pretend a puppy _____ home with you.   pet

   Here is a _____ of puppy tips.   went

2. First _____ some puppy food at the store.   fed

   A good brand might have meat and _____ in it.   get

   A puppy can be _____ three small meals a day.   eggs

3. Teach your puppy to behave _____.   yell

   Say "No" _____ your puppy makes a mistake.   when

   Never _____ at your puppy.   well

4. You can _____ your puppy learn tricks.   end

   Take one _____ at a time.   help

   Say "Good dog!" at the _____ of the day.   step

5. It is important to _____ your puppy's health.   wet

   Take your puppy to the _____.   vet

   A cold, _____ nose means your puppy is healthy.   check

6. Your puppy will need lots of _____.   bed

   A box can make a fine _____.   best

   Be your puppy's _____ friend.   rest

34   Unit 2: Short Vowel *e*

Ask your child to use **short e** words in three sentences about a pet.

Find the word in the box that completes each sentence. Be sure the word has the short sound of the vowel at the beginning of the sentence. Write the word on the line.

bat	catch	champs	chip	drops	fast
grin	hits	hot	jog	knock	mitt
stop	toss	will	win		

o 1. It is a _____, sunny day.

i 2. The heat _____ not spoil the big game.

a 3. Samantha grabs her _____ and cap.

i 4. Jon brings a ball and his _____.

o 5. They _____ quickly down the block.

o 6. Jon and Samantha _____ at the park.

o 7. They _____ the ball to get ready for the game.

i 8. They wonder if their team will _____.

a 9. Jon runs to _____ the ball.

i 10. Samantha has a big _____ on her face.

o 11. Jon tells her to _____ the ball out of the park.

i 12. She _____ the ball with a loud crack!

o 13. The ball flies up and then _____ over the wall.

a 14. Samantha runs around the bases very _____.

a 15. Samantha and Jon's team are the _____!

i 16. They get chocolate _____ ice cream as a prize.

Name _____

Unit 2: Short Vowels *a, o,* and *i* Review

Think of a word to complete each rhyme. Write the word on the line.

1. I wonder why my furry pet

   Hates to get a little _____.

2. I wonder if a red _____

   Would like to live in my den.

3. I wonder if I can _____

   Over this great big hump.

4. I wonder if I look my best

   When I wear my yellow _____.

5. I wonder why it is fun

   To play outside in the _____.

6. Why does a tiny _____

   Like to hide under a rug?

7. Would a little bear _____

   Like a bath in my tub?

8. On the table I put one cent.

   I wonder where it _____.

9. Can you jump on the bed

   Until your face turns _____?

10. Why would a _____

    Hide under your bunk?

Ask your child to choose some **short u** or **short e** words to write a rhyme.

The word **red** in each sentence stands for a word in the box. Replace **red** with the correct word in the box. Write the word on the line at the bottom of the page.

PHONICS and SPELLING

1. It's time to go to summer **red**.
2. Do you wonder why I have **red** there?
3. It's because the **red** shines every day.
4. I wear a **red** so that my head doesn't burn.
5. My cabin has a **red** to cool us off.
6. We often have a **red** race in the morning.
7. We each **red** into a big bag.
8. Then we see who can **red** the farthest.
9. Later we go to the court to **red** some tennis balls.
10. We try to get the balls to go over the **red**.
11. At lunch we have **red** and cheese sandwiches.
12. We rest for an hour before we **red** in the lake.
13. At **red** o'clock it is time for dinner.
14. Every night I go to sleep on my **red**.
15. It is not as **red** as my bed at home.
16. I can still sleep **red**, though.
17. Days at camp are the **red** days!

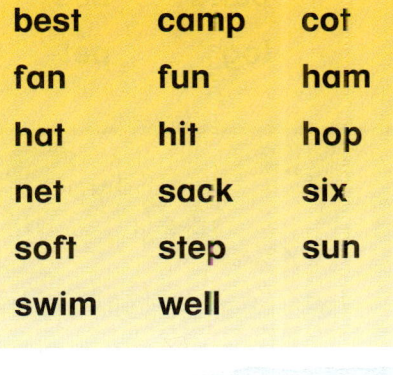

best	camp	cot
fan	fun	ham
hat	hit	hop
net	sack	six
soft	step	sun
swim	well	

1. _____ 2. _____ 3. _____
4. _____ 5. _____ 6. _____
7. _____ 8. _____ 9. _____
10. _____ 11. _____ 12. _____
13. _____ 14. _____ 15. _____
16. _____ 17. _____

Name _____

Unit 2: Spelling Words with Short Vowels

Use words from the box to make a rhyme for each picture.
Write the rhyming words on the lines beside the picture.

| band | best | bug | camp | damp | frog | grin |
| log | pet | sand | test | tug | twin | wet |

1.  _____ _____

2.  _____ _____

3.  _____ _____

4.  _____ _____

5.  _____ _____

6.  _____ _____

7.  _____ _____

Unit 2: Short Vowels Review

Ask your child to name more short vowel words that rhyme with the words on this page.

 Read the passage. Then read the sentences below it. Write the word that completes each sentence.

Fizz! Pop! Yum!

Did you ever wonder how soda pop was first made? Long ago, people drank spring water. They thought it kept them from getting sick. Some spring water has carbon dioxide in it. This is a harmless gas that makes water fizz. People liked the fizzy spring water, so scientists tried to make it in labs.

In 1772 Joseph Priestly added baking soda to plain water. The drink was just like fizzy spring water, so it was called carbonated water.

Soon drug stores sold carbonated water as a health drink. A cork in the top of each bottle kept the fizz in the water. The cork made a popping sound when it was pulled out. People began to call the drink "pop." Soon people could buy "pop" in flavors such as lemon, lime, grape, and cherry.

Today carbonated drinks are made in factories instead of in drug stores. Depending on where you live, you might call a carbonated drink "pop" or "soda." Can you think of other names for soda pop?

1. Some people thought spring water _____ them healthy.

2. Carbon dioxide is a _____.

3. Joseph Priestly _____ baking soda to water to make it fizz.

4. Carbonated water was first sold in _____ stores.

5. A cork was put in the _____ of each bottle.

Name _____

Unit 2: Reading Short Vowel Words in Context

Choose one of your favorite drinks or foods. Write an ad for this drink or food. Describe the product and tell why people should buy it. The words in the box may help you.

best	big	box
can	cup	fast
fun	get	grand
help	hot	pop
taste	thrill	zip

Ask your child to read the ad to you.

Unit 2: Writing Short Vowel Words

rake   nail   hay

Say each picture name. Complete the word if it has the **long a** sound.

RULES A vowel usually has the long sound when a consonant and **e** come after it. The **e** is silent.

When two vowels are together, the first vowel usually has the long sound. The second vowel is silent.

You can hear the **long a** sound in **rake**, **nail**, and **hay**.

1. m __ l
2. c __ n
3. p __
4. c __ p
5. l __ k
6. p __ l
7. p __ n
8. r __ n
9. r __
10. c __ p
11. s __ l
12. b __ t
13. t __ p
14. c __ n
15. w __ v
16. j __

Name _____

Unit 2: Long Vowel *a*

41

Find the word in the box that completes each question. Write the word on the line.

cake	cane
clay	hay
jay	lake
mane	paint
rays	snails
tail	trail

1. How much _____ does an elephant eat in a day?

2. Why is a blue _____ a bossy bird?

3. How much rain does it take to fill a _____?

4. Why does a _____ rise as it bakes?

5. How long does it take to _____ the White House?

6. Are some _____ slower than others?

7. Who made the first candy _____?

8. Why does a lion have a _____?

9. What makes pieces of _____ stick together?

10. How far do the sun's _____ travel into space?

11. How is a _____ different from a road?

12. How does a dog wag its _____?

Unit 2: Long Vowel *a*

Ask your child to suggest answers to some of the questions.

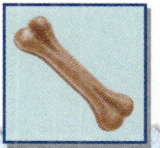  

bone   coat   bowl

Circle each **long o** word in the box. Then write the word that names each picture.

RULES A vowel usually has the long sound when a consonant and **e** come after it. The **e** is silent.

When two vowels are together, the first vowel usually has the long sound. The second vowel is silent.

You can hear the **long o** sound in **bone, coat,** and **bowl**.

boat	box	blow	cot	crow	dome	goal	got
hoe	hot	mole	mop	mow	nose	pot	robe
rod	rope	row	soap	toad	toast	toe	top

1.  _____

2. 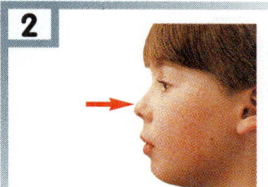 _____

3.  _____

4.  _____

5.  _____

6.  _____

7.  _____

8.  _____

9. 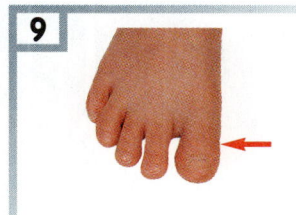 _____

10.  _____

11.  _____

12.  _____

13.  _____

14.  _____

15.  _____

16.  _____

Name _____

Unit 2: Long Vowel *o*

What did Kate do at school today? Read each sentence to find out. Circle the words with the **long o** sound. Write the words on the lines.

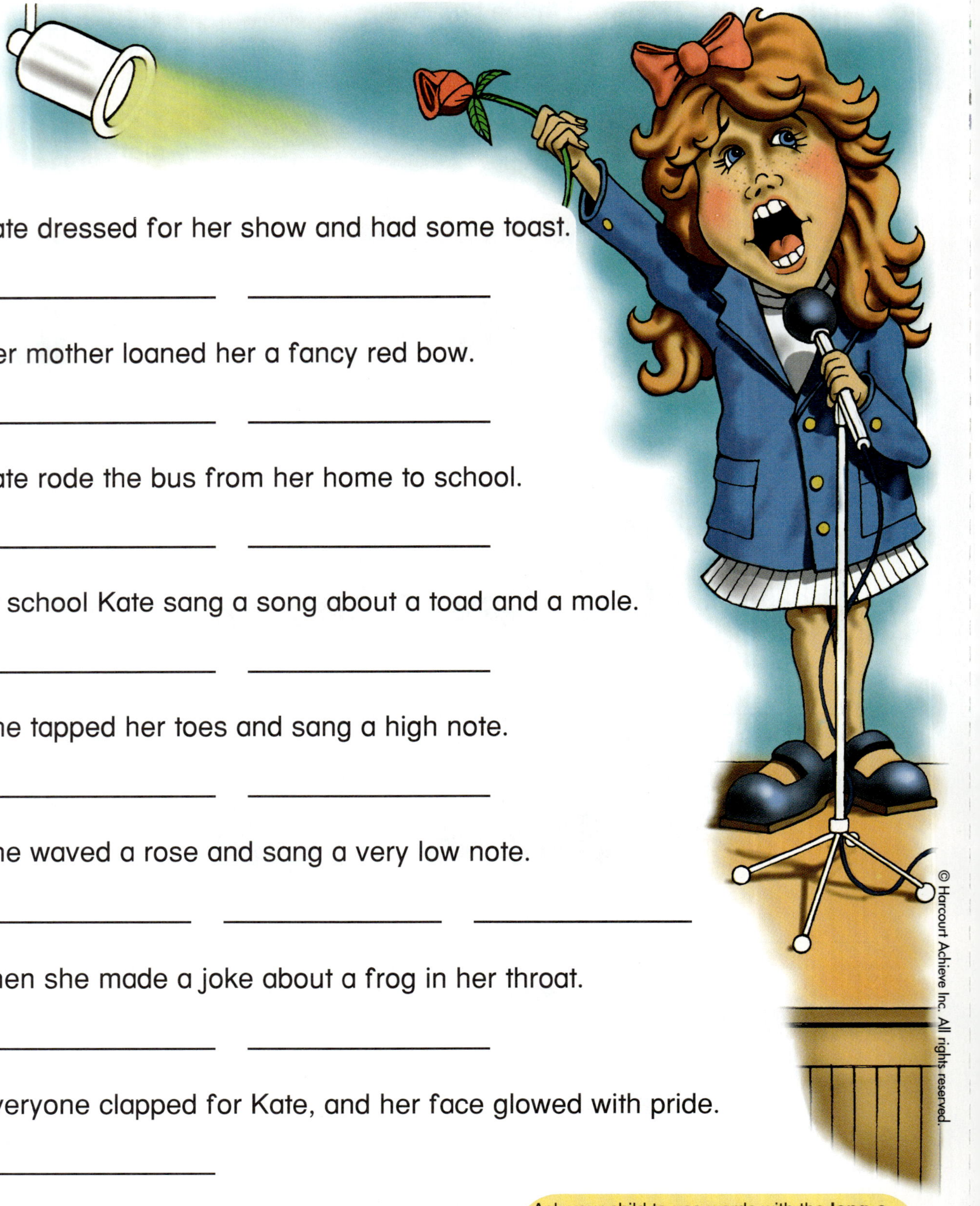

1. Kate dressed for her show and had some toast.

   _____   _____

2. Her mother loaned her a fancy red bow.

   _____   _____

3. Kate rode the bus from her home to school.

   _____   _____

4. At school Kate sang a song about a toad and a mole.

   _____   _____

5. She tapped her toes and sang a high note.

   _____   _____

6. She waved a rose and sang a very low note.

   _____   _____   _____

7. Then she made a joke about a frog in her throat.

   _____   _____

8. Everyone clapped for Kate, and her face glowed with pride.

   _____

44 Unit 2: Long Vowel *o*

Ask your child to use words with the **long o** sound to write another sentence about Kate's day at school.

kite   tie   light

Circle the word that names each picture.
Write the word on the line.

RULES A vowel usually has the long sound when a consonant and **e** come after it. The **e** is silent.

When two vowels are together, the first vowel usually has the long sound. The second vowel is silent.

When the vowel **i** is followed by **gh**, the **i** usually has the long sound. The **g** and **h** are silent.

You can hear the **long i** sound in **kite**, **tie**, and **light**.

1.
pipe
pig
pine

2.
pile
pipe
pie

3.
hill
hike
hitch

4.
nail
night
nice

5.
bit
boat
bike

6.
die
did
dice

7.
vet
vine
visit

8.
tiles
toads
tights

9.
tie
tip
tide

10.
thigh
that
thin

11.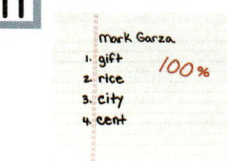
rig
right
rein

12.
lie
lit
life

Name _____

Unit 2: Long Vowel *i*   **45**

Find the word in the box that answers each question. Write the word on the line.

dime	high	ice	lime	mice	night	nine	pie
pine	prize	right	sigh	sight	smile	tight	wide

1. What coin is worth ten cents? _____
2. What is the opposite of *day*? _____
3. What is another word for *correct*? _____
4. What is more than one mouse? _____
5. What is the opposite of *loose*? _____
6. What is a sound you might make when you're sad? _____
7. What kind of dessert has a crust? _____
8. What is something you win? _____
9. What is the opposite of *low*? _____
10. What is a name for a kind of green fruit? _____
11. What is frozen water? _____
12. What is on a happy face? _____
13. What is the opposite of *narrow*? _____
14. What is the sum of four plus five? _____
15. What kind of tree has cones? _____
16. What sense lets us see? _____

Ask your child to use some words from the box to write two-line rhymes.

Unit 2: Long Vowel *i*

colt

child

Say each picture name. Write **o** if you hear the **long o** sound. Write **i** if you hear the **long i** sound.

RULE Some words with only one vowel have the long sound instead of the short sound. You can hear the **long o** sound in **colt** and the **long i** sound in **child**.

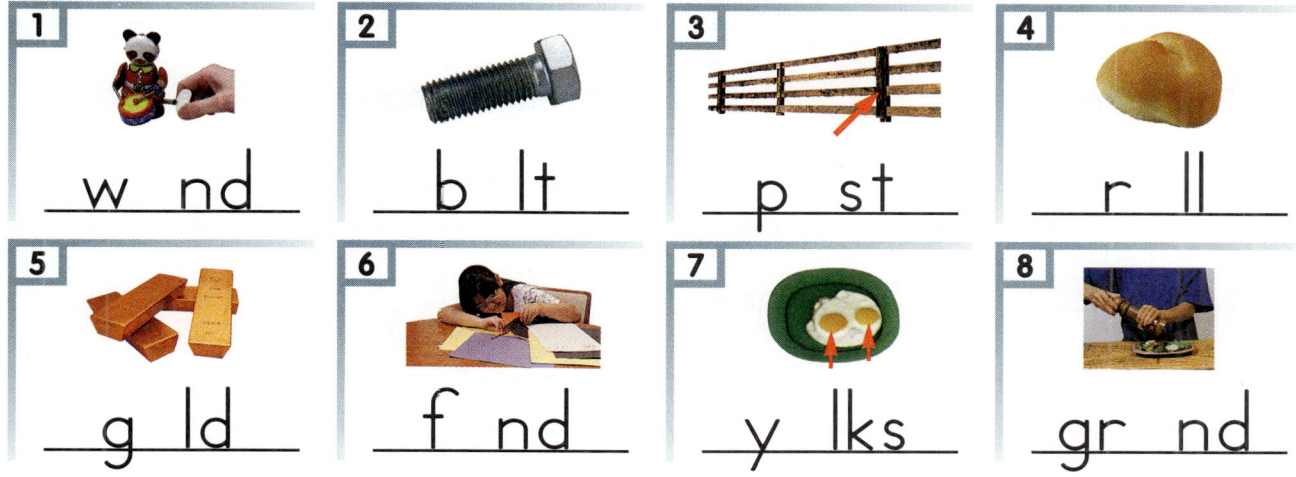

1. w___nd
2. b___lt
3. p___st
4. ___r___ll
5. g___ld
6. f___nd
7. y___lks
8. gr___nd

Find the word in the box that completes each sentence. Write the word on the line.

| cold   colt   folk   kind   mild   signs   stroll   wild |

9. I wonder if the weather will be _____ or hot tomorrow.

10. I obey all the traffic _____ when I ride my bike.

11. Let's go for a _____ in the park.

12. Maria likes spicy food, but I like _____ food.

13. What _____ of food do you like?

14. The Russian _____ dancers wore colorful costumes.

15. Hikers should not feed _____ animals.

16. Our mare had a little _____ yesterday.

Name _____

Unit 2: Exceptions for Vowels *o* and *i*

Choose the word that completes each sentence. Write the word on the line.

1. Every morning I drink a whole _____ of milk.   rolls

   Mom makes sweet _____ for breakfast.   pint

2. I don't have to be _____ to do my chores.   told

   I _____ the laundry and then go outside.   fold

3. I don't _____ the snow.   cold

   The _____ air feels good on my face.   mind

4. First I _____ the pail and some hay.   find

   Our frisky _____ is glad to see me.   colt

5. The little horse is the color of _____.   post

   He gallops to the fence _____.   gold

6. The colt is not _____ anymore.   hold

   I _____ the pail while he eats.   wild

7. We go for a _____ down the road.   most

   Do you wonder what I like to do _____?   stroll

8. I like to be _____ to our animals.   old

   I care for the young ones and the _____ ones.   kind

48 Unit 2: Exceptions for Vowels *o* and *i*

Ask your child to find other **long o** and **long i** words in the sentences.

Each word in the box is in the puzzle. Find and circle each word. Words can go across, down, or at a slant. Then write each word in the correct column below.

away	bold	child	day	flow
lie	load	mail	might	mild
rice	say	space	those	toe

```
m  s  j  d  m  a  i  l  u
i  p  a  a  w  a  y  o  w
g  a  f  y  l  i  e  a  r
h  c  l  c  h  i  l  d  i
t  e  o  t  h  o  s  e  c
q  x  w  m  i  l  d  b  e
k  b  o  l  d  t  o  e  g
```

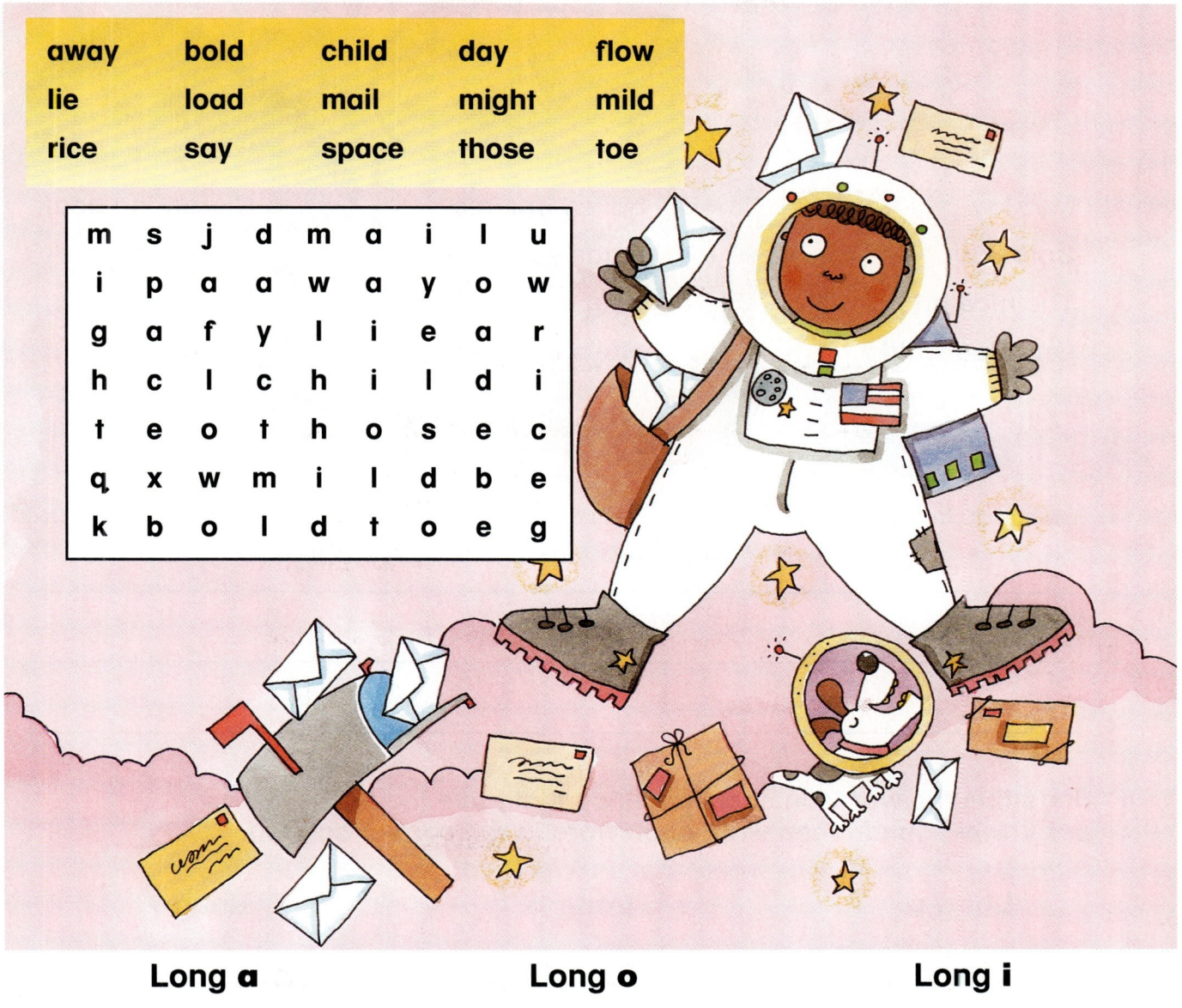

Long a   **Long o**   **Long i**

_____   _____   _____

_____   _____   _____

_____   _____   _____

_____   _____   _____

_____   _____   _____

Name _____

Unit 2: Long Vowels *a*, *o*, and *i* Review

Combine one phrase from each box to make four sentences. Use each phrase only once. Write the sentences on the lines below.

A.
- Ms. Jay
- Bold Joe
- The nice bride
- Grandpa Gold

B.
- baked one pie
- made some toast
- rides a bike
- plays our game

C.
- on the boat.
- at home.
- in the rain.
- at night.

1. _____
2. _____
3. _____
4. _____

Underline the words in each sentence that have the **long a, o,** or **i** vowel sound. Then write each word in the correct column.

Long a	Long o	Long i
_____	_____	_____
_____	_____	_____
_____	_____	_____
_____	_____	_____
_____	_____	_____

Unit 2: Long Vowels *a, o,* and *i* Review

Ask your child to combine different phrases to create new sentences.

cube   **flute**   **blue**

Say each picture name. Complete the word if it has the **long u** sound.

RULES A vowel usually has the long sound when a consonant and **e** come after it. The **e** is silent.

When two vowels are together in a word, the first vowel usually has the long sound. The second vowel is silent.

You can hear the **long u** sound in **cube**, **flute**, and **blue**.

1. t___b
2. bl___
3. c___b
4. pr___n
5. pl___m
6. b___g
7. m___l
8. h___g
9. gl___
10. J___n
11. d___ck
12. f___s
13. d___n
14. t___b
15. t___n
16. j___g

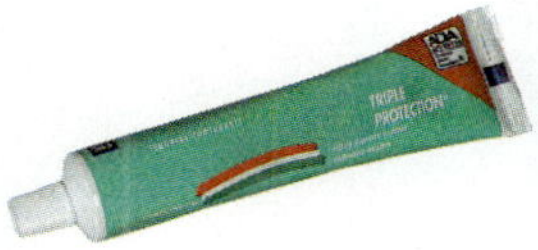

Name _____

Unit 2: Long Vowel **u**

The underlined word in each sentence does not make sense. Find a word in the box that does make sense. Write it on the line. **Hint:** The correct word begins like the underlined word.

1. Sue and <u>Like</u> want to put on a show. _____
2. At first they don't have a <u>clap</u> how to begin. _____
3. They wonder what to <u>unit</u> for a stage. _____
4. Then Sue finds a <u>hope</u> box. _____
5. It is shaped like a <u>cab</u>. _____
6. Sue covers the box with a <u>blow</u> cloth. _____
7. Luke wants to play a <u>take</u> in the show. _____
8. He finds a long cardboard <u>toad</u>. _____
9. Luke thinks it will make a great <u>flap</u>. _____
10. Sue and Luke use <u>glow</u> to make masks. _____
11. Sue is a bear with a <u>cave</u> face. _____
12. Luke is a funny <u>mail</u>. _____
13. All the children come to watch on one <u>Josh</u> day. _____
14. No one is <u>ride</u>. Everyone claps politely. _____

blue
clue
cube
cute
flute
glue
huge
June
Luke
mule
rude
tube
tune
use

Unit 2: Long Vowel *u*

AT HOME

Ask your child to think of other names that have the **long *u*** sound. Prompt your child for first and last names.

leaf   bee

Circle the word that names each picture. Write the word on the line.

RULE When two vowels are together, the first vowel usually has the long sound. The second vowel is silent. You can hear the **long e** sound in **leaf** and **bee**.

1.  ten / team / tea

2.  send / soap / seed

3.  pest / peas / past

4. 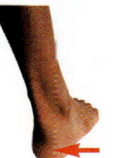 heel / hail / heat

5.  bend / bean / beak

6.  peach / peek / pack

7.  jet / jeans / jeep

8.  leak / like / luck

9. 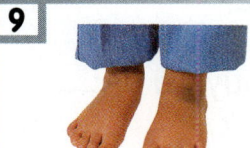 fell / fear / feet

10.  quiet / queen / quit

11.  seal / seem / sell

12.  weak / went / weed

13.  meet / meal / meat

14.  knew / knee / kneel

15.  leash / lash / lean

Name _____

Unit 2: Long Vowel *e*

Read each sentence and the words below it. Write the two words that will complete the sentence.

1. What will _____ _____ at the park?
   Lee   bean   see

2. Whom will he _____ on the _____?
   street   meet   wheat

3. A man drives by in a _____ _____.
   jeep   sweep   neat

4. A _____ buzzes in a _____.
   peace   bee   tree

5. Birds in a nest _____ and _____.
   beet   cheep   peep

6. Two girls _____ a picnic _____.
   meal   eat   beak

7. Lee buys a _____ _____.
   weak   treat   sweet

8. A soccer _____ rests near a _____.
   stream   queen   team

9. Lee _____ his friend _____.
   sees   Neal   seal

10. They _____ to _____ the ducks.
    need   feed   leap

11. The pond looks like the _____ blue _____.
    sea   knee   deep

12. Lee and Neal will _____ at the park next _____.
    week   seem   meet

54   Unit 2: Long Vowel *e*

Ask your child to write sentences with some of the words that don't fit in the sentences above.

Write the name of each picture.

Circle each word that has the long e or the long u sound.

13. nut   true   huge   club   rude   blue
14. green net   real   glee   fell   steam
15. cheap speed   helmet street free   stem
16. rule   hut   hug   due   plume   tube
17. pet   pea   agree   dream   cheek   check
18. prune fuel   fun   tune   dull   use

Name _____

Unit 2: Long Vowels *u* and *e* Review

Write **yes** or **no** to answer each question. Then underline the **long u** and **long e** words in the questions. Write the **long u** and **long e** words in the columns below.

1. Is a beet blue? _____
2. Is a prune something to eat? _____
3. Is a bee huge? _____
4. Can a sheep climb a tree? _____
5. Does a mule drink iced tea? _____
6. Is glue used to play a tune? _____
7. Do some children feel heat in June? _____
8. Is a little seal called a flute? _____
9. Could a queen wear a plume on her crown? _____
10. Is a sugar cube sweet? _____

Long u   **Long e**

_____ _____   _____ _____

_____ _____   _____ _____

_____ _____   _____ _____

_____ _____   _____ _____

_____   _____

Ask your child to read the questions to you so that you can answer them.

Find the word in the box that names each picture. Write the word on the line. Then say the word and listen for the number of syllables. Write the word in the correct column below.

RULE Words are made of small parts called **syllables**. Each syllable has one vowel sound. A word can have one or more syllables.

| ambulance | desk | hose | lemon | parachute | pot |
| puppet | robin | train | violin | volcano | wagon |

1. _____ 
2. _____ 
3. _____ 
4. _____ 
5. _____ 
6. _____ 
7. _____ 
8. _____ 
9. _____ 
10. _____ 
11. _____ 
12. _____

One Syllable　　　　**Two Syllables**　　　　**Three Syllables**

_____　　_____　　_____

_____　　_____　　_____

_____　　_____　　_____

_____　　_____　　_____

Name _____

Unit 2: Syllables 57

Use the words in the box to answer the riddles. Use one-syllable words for the first set of riddles. Use two-syllable words for the second set and three-syllable words for the third set.

| banana | boat | cactus | five | kangaroo | kitten |
| leaf | octopus | tiger | umbrella | vest | zipper |

1. It rhymes with *nest*.
   It's something you can wear.

   It's a _____.

2. It begins with the letter *l*.
   It's found on a tree.

   It's a _____.

3. It rhymes with *hive*.
   It's one more than four.

   It's _____.

4. It rhymes with *goat*.
   It travels on water.

   It's a _____.

5. It can be on a jacket.
   It moves up and down.

   It's a _____.

6. It is a desert plant.
   It might stick you.

   It's a _____.

7. It is soft and purrs.
   It's a baby cat.

   It's a _____.

8. It has stripes and roars.
   It's a big cat.

   It's a _____.

9. It is an animal that hops.
   It carries its baby in a pouch.

   It's a _____.

10. It has eight arms.
    It lives in the sea.

    It's an _____.

11. It is good to have in the rain.
    It has a handle and opens wide.

    It's an _____.

12. It is a yellow fruit.
    It grows in a bunch.

    It's a _____.

Have your child point out the two-syllable words in the riddles.

58 Unit 2: Syllables

Read each sentence. Unscramble the words in dark print. Then write the correct word on the line. The words in the box may help you.

blue	bone	jay	jeep	kite	lime
midnight	nose	pane	peace	queen	rain
tie	toast	toe	tow	tube	

1. I wonder how high I can fly this **tiek**. _____
2. I wonder why a dog likes to chew on a **nebo**. _____
3. I wonder how they get toothpaste into a **bute**. _____
4. I wonder why the sky is **elbu**. _____
5. A **neuqe** sits on a throne and wears a crown. _____
6. Cinderella had to be home by **tignidmh**. _____
7. A **meli** is bright green. _____
8. A **ajy** is a bird with blue feathers. _____
9. Mr. Ono will **wto** our truck to the garage. _____
10. The ball hit the window and broke a **neap**. _____
11. Can you use this ribbon to **ite** a bow? _____
12. The word **epej** rhymes with *sheep*. _____
13. Your **onse** is in the center of your face. _____
14. We should all work for **ceepa** on Earth. _____
15. Can it really **niar** cats and dogs? _____
16. Eggs and **atsot** are popular breakfast foods. _____
17. Ouch! I stubbed my **oet**! _____

Name _____

Unit 2: Spelling Words with Long Vowels

Find the word in the box that matches each clue.
Write the word in the puzzle.

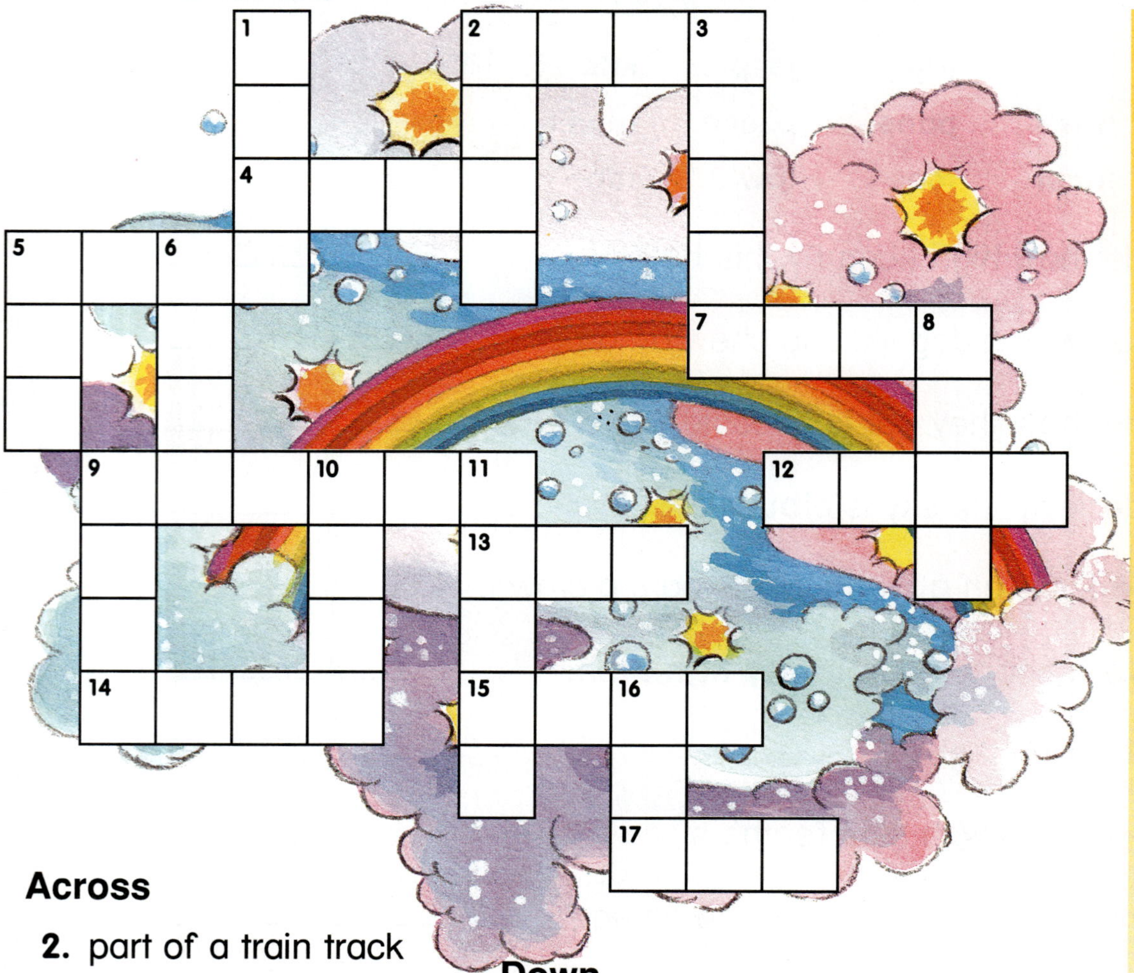

dime
eat
game
glue
hope
hoe
huge
ice
leap
light
night
pie
rail
rose
rule
sail
seal
season
soap
toad

Across

2. part of a train track
4. a furry sea mammal
5. very large
7. an animal that is like a frog
9. summer, winter, fall, or spring
12. something you play
13. frozen water
14. to jump
15. to wish
17. to chew and swallow

Down

1. a kind of flower
2. something to obey
3. not heavy
5. a garden tool
6. something that sticks like paste
8. a ten-cent coin
9. the boat part that is made of cloth
10. something for washing your hands
11. opposite of *day*
16. a dessert that has a crust

AT HOME

With your child, take turns naming words that rhyme with the words in the box.

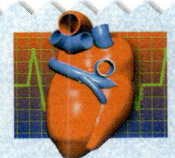

PHONICS and READING

Read the letter to Dr. Helpful and the doctor's answer. Then read the sentences at the bottom of the page. Write the word that completes each sentence.

Dear Dr. Helpful,

I am nine years old. I wonder how I can keep myself healthy. I seem to get many colds each winter. Are there any rules that I can follow? I want to feel good all the time.

Sincerely,
Brandon Nye

Dear Brandon,

No one feels good all the time. Everyone gets a cold once in a while. Here are some rules to help you. If you follow them, you will feel good most of the time.

First, eat three main meals a day. Choose a wide range of foods. Meat is good for you. You also need to eat lots of leafy, green vegetables. It is all right to have fruit for a snack.

Next, you need to keep active. Go outside and play. Skating, riding a bike, and hiking are good kinds of exercise. You can also exercise while you help at home. It takes lots of energy to rake leaves!

Finally, be sure you get a good night's sleep. Rest is important for a growing child.

If you follow these rules, you will have a healthy glow!

Yours in good health,
Dr. I. M. Helpful

1. Brandon had lots of _____ each winter.

2. The doctor gave Brandon a set of _____ to help him stay healthy.

3. A healthy meal has a wide _____ of foods.

4. It is important to eat lots of _____, green vegetables.

5. Every _____ needs plenty of rest each night.

Name _____

Unit 2: Reading Long Vowel Words in Context

What rules do you follow to keep healthy? Write a letter to the girl in the picture. Tell her what she can do to keep from getting too many colds. The words in the box may help you.

PHONICS and WRITING

eat	feel	fine	home	kind
meal	mind	most	night	nose
pain	right	sleep	use	weak

Circle the word that names each picture. Write the word on the line.

Unit 2 CHECK-UP

1
can
cane
cone
came

_____

2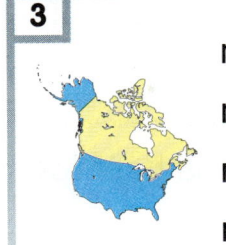
child
chick
wild
chill

_____

3
mop
main
map
man

_____

4
top
tap
tape
tip

_____

5
hat
huge
hut
hue

_____

6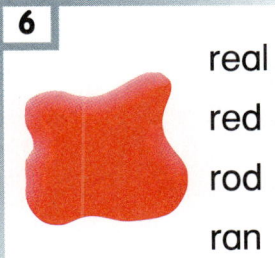
real
red
rod
ran

_____

7
cot
cat
coat
coal

_____

8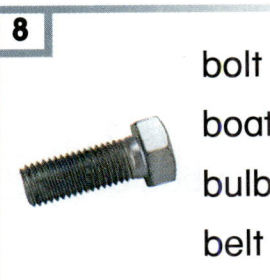
bolt
boat
bulb
belt

_____

9
bit
bike
bake
book

_____

10
dune
dine
duck
done

_____

11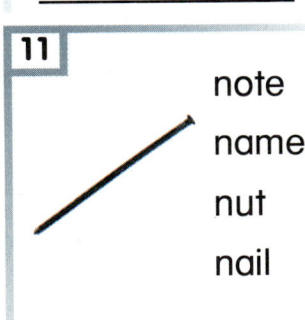
note
name
nut
nail

_____

12
fine
find
fin
file

_____

13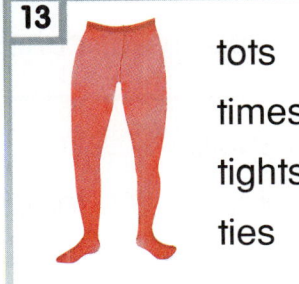
tots
times
tights
ties

_____

14
jam
jay
joy
jar

_____

15
roll
rail
rule
rock

_____

16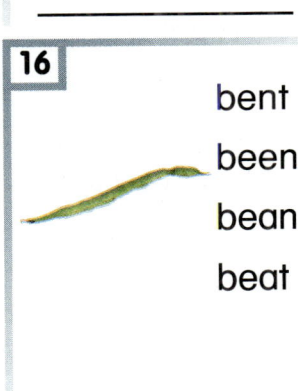
bent
been
bean
beat

_____

Name _____

Unit 2 CHECK-UP — Fill in the circle next to the word that completes each sentence.

1. I wonder who owns that _____ puppy. ○ cut ○ cube ○ cute ○ coat

2. I wonder which _____ is best for me. ○ pit ○ pet ○ pat ○ pot

3. Ava's dog always wags his _____. ○ toad ○ tag ○ tail ○ tune

4. Would you trade your favorite book for a bag of _____? ○ cold ○ most ○ colt ○ gold

5. It's fun to _____ on the trail through the woods. ○ hike ○ hit ○ hail ○ hot

6. Leave now so that you don't _____ the party. ○ mitt ○ miss ○ mess ○ mice

7. Our football _____ won the big game. ○ team ○ time ○ tea ○ tent

8. Wear a _____ to keep your head warm. ○ cup ○ cat ○ cap ○ cane

9. Be sure to _____ the door when you leave. ○ luck ○ lick ○ black ○ lock

10. I use a _____ to dig in the garden. ○ hoe ○ hay ○ huge ○ high

Unit 2: Assessing Short and Long Vowels

UNIT 3
A Dream Away
Consonant Blends and Digraphs, Silent Consonants

Dream

I dreamed
a garden
in every home

tomatoes
grew in
office windows

people greeted
each other
with flowers

no school
or church was
without a garden

everybody
had a green
thumb

and cars
were a thing
of the past

Francisco X. Alarcón

Think About It

What does the speaker in the poem wish for?
What do you wish for?

Dear Family of _____,

Your child will be learning about consonant blends, such as *sk* and *fl*; consonant digraphs, such as *ch* and *wh*; and silent consonants, such as the *w* in *wr*. Your child will be using these skills to read about hopes and dreams. Here are some activities you can do together.

- Make a set of four flash cards, writing one consonant digraph on each card (*ch, wh, sh, th*). Make up sentences using words with these sounds, such as *I can whistle* and *I will brush my teeth*. Have your child hold up the appropriate card every time you say a word with the sound of that consonant digraph.
- Make a "hope" chest from an old shoebox. Give your child pieces of paper on which to write things he or she hopes to do one day. Encourage your child to identify words with blends and digraphs.
- Help your child make up sentences using as many words as possible with the same silent consonant, such as *Nancy knew a knitting knight* or *The lamb needs a comb to get the crumbs out of its wool.*

LIBRARY LINK

You might like to visit the library and find the book the *Nighttime Chauffeur* by Carly Simon. Read it with your child.

Estimada familia de _____,

Su niño o niña aprenderá combinaciones de consonantes en inglés, tales como *sk* y *fl*, las consonantes *ch* y *wh*, además de las consonantes "silenciosas" como la *w* en *wr*. Su niño o niña usará estos conocimientos en su lectura sobre esperanzas y ensueños. Algunas actividades que usted y su niño o niña pueden hacer en inglés aparecen a continuación.

- Haga un conjunto de cuatro tarjetas o láminas con cada una de las siguientes consonantes escritas en las tarjetas: *ch, wh, sh, th*. Construya oraciones que tengan palabras con estas consonantes, tales como *"I can whistle"* y *"I will brush my teeth"*. Pídale a su niño o niña que muestre en alto la tarjeta correspondiente cada vez que usted diga una palabra con el sonido de esas consonantes.
- Conviertan una caja de zapatos en un baúl de tesoro. Dele a su niño o niña pedazos de papel en los cuales él o ella pueda escribir lo que quisiera hacer algún día. Aliente a su niño o niña a que identifique las palabras con las combinaciones de consonantes.
- Ayude a su niño o niña a construir oraciones que usen tantas palabras como sea posible con las mismas consonantes "silenciosas", tales como *"Nancy knew a knitting knight"* o *"The lamb needs a comb to get the crumbs out of its wool"*.

 scarf  skates  smoke squirrel

Find the word in the box that names each picture. Write the word on the line. Then circle the **s** blend in each word.

RULE A **consonant blend** is two or more consonants that are together. The sounds blend together. Each sound is heard. You can hear a two-letter **s** blend at the beginning of **scarf, skates, smoke,** and **squirrel**.

| scale | score | skunk | smile | snail | snake |
| spill | squash | squeeze | star | stove | swim |

1.  scale
2.  skunk
3.  squeeze
4.  swim
5.  smile
6.  snake
7.  spill
8.  stove
9.  score
10.  star
11.  snail
12.  squash

Unit 3: Initial **s** Blends

splash **string**

Circle the word that names each picture.
Write the word on the line.

RULE Some **consonant blends** have three consonants. You can hear an **s** blend with three letters at the beginning of **splash** and **string**.

1.
screen
scram
scream
_____

2.
spray
sprout
sprite
_____

3.
streak
straw
strange
_____

4.
sprint
spread
sprang
_____

5.
strap
strike
stripe
_____

6.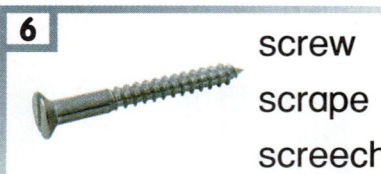
screw
scrape
screech
_____

7.
screw
scratch
scrub
_____

8.
spring
sprain
spread
_____

9.
stroll
strong
string
_____

Find the word in the box that completes each sentence.
Write the word on the line.

scratch
splash
stray
stream
stretch

10. I dream about living beside a _____ in the woods.

11. Every afternoon I would _____ out for a nap.

12. I would find a _____ kitten and take good care of it.

13. I would teach it not to _____ or hiss.

14. We would sit and watch the fish _____ in the water.

Point to some of the **s** blend words on the page. Use each word in a sentence. Have your child do the same.

crab   drum   frog   grapes

Say each picture name. Write the **r** blend on the line to complete the word.

RULE Remember that a **consonant blend** is two or more consonants that are together. You can hear an **r** blend at the beginning of **crab, drum, frog,** and **grapes**.

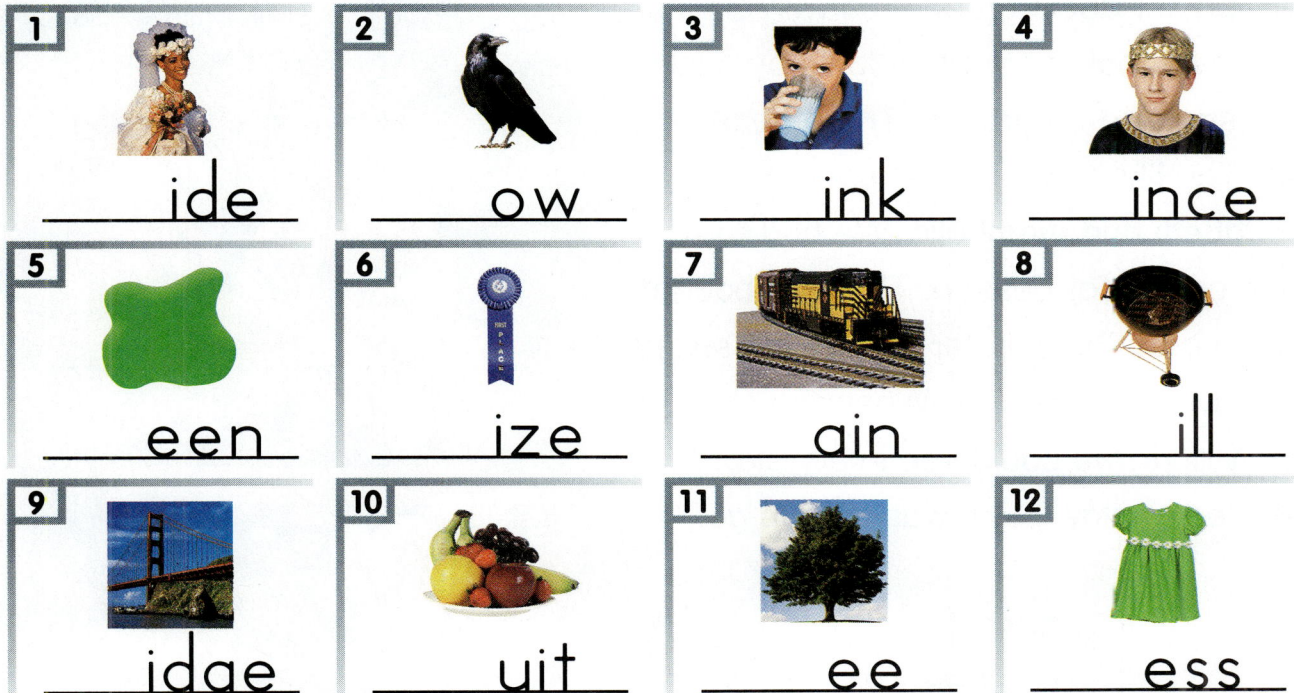

1. ___ide
2. ___ow
3. ___ink
4. ___ince
5. ___een
6. ___ize
7. ___ain
8. ___ill
9. ___idge
10. ___uit
11. ___ee
12. ___ess

Circle the word that completes each sentence. Write the word on the line.

13. Dana's dream is to play a _____ piano.   grown   grand
14. I hope I can keep in touch with my _____.   friends   frills
15. I wish that dress had a lower _____.   praise   price
16. It would be great to _____ a fine painting.   crust   create
17. I'd like to feel the cool ocean _____.   bread   breeze
18. Todd wants to learn how to do magic _____.   tricks   tracks

Name _____

Unit 3: Initial *r* Blends

Read the story. Find and circle the words that begin with s blends. Next, find and underline the words that begin with r blends. Then write each word in the correct column.

I dreamed of a special trip with my grandmother. One spring day we traveled to Spain. People greeted us with smiles. Then we took a train to a town by a lake. We snacked on grapes. The breeze smelled like flowers! For lunch we ate spaghetti and meatballs. We had fruit with cream for dessert. Then we bought some great hats. Later we fed the swans that swam in the lake. When the sky grew dark, we could see every star. I wanted to stay, but it was time to go.

s Blends		r Blends	
_____	_____	_____	_____
_____	_____	_____	_____
_____	_____	_____	_____
_____	_____	_____	_____
_____	_____	_____	_____
_____	_____	_____	_____

Help your child make a list of foods that begin with s blends and r blends. Use grocery ads to help.

fl ag   tw elve

The words at the left name the pictures in each row. Write each word under its picture. Then circle the **l** or **tw** blend in each word.

RULE Remember that a **consonant blend** is two or more consonants that are together in a word. The sounds blend together, but each sound is heard. You can hear an **l** blend at the beginning of **flag** and a **tw** blend at the beginning of **twelve**.

slip
twins
clock
flute

1.  _____
2.  _____
3.  _____
4.  _____

twenty
flower
globe
black

5. 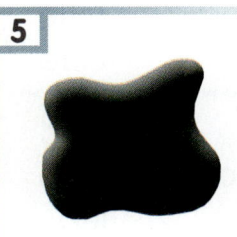 _____
6.  _____
7.  _____
8.  _____

plum
glass
twig
cloud

9.  _____
10.  _____
11. 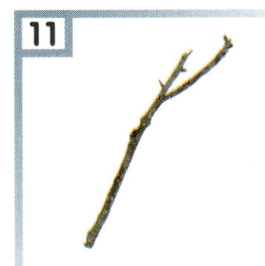 _____
12.  _____

blouse
twirl
plate
slide

13.  _____
14.  _____
15.  _____
16.  _____

Name _____

Unit 3: Initial *l* and *tw* Blends

Circle the word that completes each sentence. Then write the word on the line.

1. I dreamed of soft _____ of snow.   flakes / brakes / cakes

2. Snow fell from gray _____.   loud / blocks / clouds

3. All the children put on their _____.   doves / gloves / globes

4. Each child had a _____ scarf to wear.   blue / glue / clue

5. Everyone had a wooden _____ to ride.   sled / step / led

6. Each child slid down the hill _____.   twig / slice / twice

7. Then a _____ flew overhead.   plane / plant / pane

8. It dropped _____ lunches for the children.   twist / twelve / train

9. Everyone was _____ to have the wonderful food.   glass / glad / flag

10. They were happy to _____ all day.   play / plate / plum

72   Unit 3: Reading Words with Initial *l* and *tw* Blends in Context

Read several of the answer choices and ask your child to name a rhyming word for each.

lamp   list

Read each clue and look at the picture. Use a word from the box to complete the answer. Write the word on the line.

RULE A **consonant blend** can also come at the end of a word. You can hear a consonant blend at the end of **lamp** and **list**.

| band | cent | hand | lamp | mask |
| nest | quilt | tent | vest | wasp |

1 I make music.

I am a _____.

2 I am fun to camp in.

I am a _____.

3 I look good with a shirt.

I am a _____.

4 I hold a bird's eggs.

I am a _____.

5 I light up a room.

I am a _____.

6 I cover a face.

I am a _____.

7 I keep people warm.

I am a _____.

8 I might sting you.

I am a _____.

9 I am equal to one penny.

I am a _____.

10 I have fingers.

I am a _____.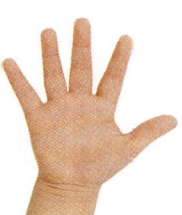

Name _____

Unit 3: Final Blends

Circle the word that completes each sentence. Write the word on the line.

1. Trent makes a _____ of jobs he could have when he grows up.
   - lisp
   - list
   - lies

2. Trent dreams of playing drums in a _____.
   - band
   - bank
   - back

3. He could wear a _____ if he worked at a lumber mill.
   - vent
   - vet
   - vest

4. He could also wear a tool _____.
   - belt
   - bell
   - best

5. When Trent smells the sweet _____ of flowers, he wants to be a florist.
   - scent
   - spent
   - scene

6. Trent likes to _____, so maybe he'll be a park ranger.
   - cast
   - came
   - camp

7. Maybe Trent will live in the _____ and ride horses.
   - Wet
   - West
   - Went

8. Trent thinks he should _____ his teacher for ideas.
   - ache
   - ask
   - asp

9. The teacher holds Trent's _____ in hers.
   - had
   - hand
   - hang

10. She says, "You have lots of time to find the job that is _____ for you."
    - bell
    - bets
    - best

Unit 3: Final Blends

AT HOME Read each correct answer and have your child say a word that rhymes with it.

Find the word in the box that matches each clue. Write the word. Then use the shaded letters to answer the riddle at the bottom of the page.

| cent | cloud | frog | hand | play | prize |
| skunk | spoon | spring | twice | west | |

1. was once a tadpole
2. rhymes with *moon*
3. what rain falls from
4. an animal with a stripe down its back
5. two times
6. opposite of *east*
7. season after winter
8. the palm, fingers, and thumb
9. less than a nickel
10. what the winner gets
11. opposite of *work*

How did the lamb get to the moon?

On a _____ _____

Name _____

Unit 3: Initial and Final Blends Review

Look at each birdhouse. Find the two words in the box that have the blend on the birdhouse. Write the words in the birdhouse. Then write another word with the same blend.

globe	twig	land	bolt	dream	space
flag	glass	scream	skate	spice	drink
send	skip	flute	belt	twelve	scrub

Unit 3: Initial and Final Blends Review

Ask your child to use one group of words to make up sentences.

  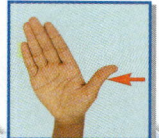 

chair   shoe   thumb   whale

Find the word in the box that names each picture. Write the word on the line. Then circle the letters that stand for the **first** sound in each word.

RULE A **consonant digraph** is two or more consonants that are together. They stand for only one sound. You can hear a consonant digraph at the beginning of **chair**, **shoe**, **thumb**, and **whale**.

| cheek | chin | sheep | ship |
| them | thirteen | wheat | wheel |

1.  _____
2.  _____
3.  _____
4.  _____
5. 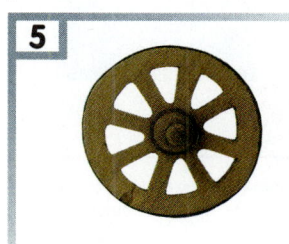 _____
6.  _____
7.  _____
8.  _____

Find the word in the box that completes each sentence. Write the word on the line.

9. I hope I have the _____ to raise horses one day.

10. My horses would have thick, _____ coats.

11. I would train my horses and ride them in horse _____.

12. I would never _____ them or yell at them.

13. They would learn to come when I _____ for them.

14. I think _____ I will make a wonderful rancher!

chance
shiny
shows
that
whip
whistled

Name _____

Unit 3: Initial Consonant Digraphs **ch, sh, th,** and **wh**

77

orchid   chef

Find the word at the left that names each picture. Write the word on the line.

RULE The consonant digraph **ch** usually stands for the sound you hear at the beginning of **chair**. It can also stand for the **k** sound you hear in **orchid** and the **sh** sound you hear in **chef**.

chandelier
chauffeur
orchestra

1.
_____

2.
_____

3.
_____

chemicals
parachute
chef

4.
_____

5.
_____

6.
_____

chorus
chute
chemist

7.
_____

8.
_____

9.
_____

Circle the word in each sentence that has a ch digraph. Then circle the correct sound for ch at the right.

10. Dave dreams of studying monarch butterflies.   k   sh
11. Kara sang out in the mountains and heard an echo.   k   sh
12. Ben's uncle has a bushy mustache.   k   sh
13. Jennifer wants to build big machines when she grows up.   k   sh
14. The doctor can cure your aches and pains.   k   sh

Find words in newspapers, magazines, and books that have **ch**. Have your child identify which sound the letters **ch** stand for.

Unit 3: Variant Sounds of *ch*

phone   **laugh**

Draw a line to match each picture to its name. Write each word under its picture. Then circle the two letters that stand for the **f** sound in each word you wrote.

RULE The consonant digraphs **ph** and **gh** can stand for the **f** sound. You can hear the digraphs **ph** and **gh** in **phone** and **laugh**.

1. photograph

4. rough

2. dolphin

5. elephant

3. cough

6. trophy

Circle the word that completes each sentence. Write the word on the line.

7. In (phonics, phrased) we learn the sounds that letters stand for. _____

8. I wish this meat were not so (turf, tough). _____

9. Alex knows all the letters in the Russian (autograph, alphabet). _____

10. Are ten push-ups (elephant, enough) for your age group? _____

11. I picked up the (phone, fun) and called my friend. _____

Name _____

Circle the word that completes each sentence. Write the word on the line.

1. _____ were the gardens that you dreamed about?

   Wheat
   Where
   Share

2. The gardens were growing in sunny and _____ spots.

   thread
   shaky
   shady

3. Everybody had a green _____.

   thumb
   thunder
   thick

4. A _____ could reach out the window to pick vegetables.

   chew
   chef
   chop

5. My plants were in the ABC order of the _____.

   photograph
   microphone
   alphabet

6. My garden made people _____.

   laugh
   rough
   graph

7. I won a _____ for the funniest garden.

   nephew
   gopher
   trophy

8. I saw one garden in the _____ of the letter *L*.

   shape
   shave
   sheep

9. Another garden was planted in the shape of a _____.

   wheel
   white
   while

10. No _____ or parent was hungry.

    chin
    child
    chimney

80 Unit 3: Reading Words with Consonant Digraphs in Context

AT HOME Have your child circle the digraphs in each answer choice.

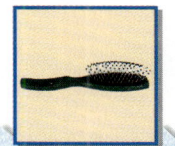 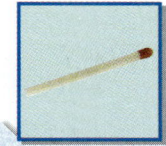

brush   match

Say each picture name and write it on the line. Then circle the letters that stand for the **last** sound in each word.

> **RULE** Consonant **digraphs** come at the end of many words. Some have three letters. You can hear a consonant digraph at the end of **brush** and **match**.

1.  _____
2.  _____
3.  _____
4.  _____
5.  _____
6. 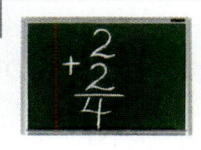 _____
7.  _____
8.  _____

Find the word in the box that completes each sentence. Write it in the crossword puzzle.

bank	beach
chick	cloth
patch	ranch
ring	sing

Across

1. I keep my money in a piggy _____.
2. A _____ hatches from an egg.
4. We raise sheep and horses on our _____.
5. We can _____ a song about spring.
6. The pirate wears a _____ over his eye.

Down

1. I built a sand castle at the _____.
3. I am buying the pink _____ to make pants.
4. The bride has a diamond _____ on her finger.

Name _____

Unit 3: Final Consonant Digraphs **ch, sh, th, ck, ng, nk,** and **tch**

81

Underline each word that contains the consonant digraph listed at the beginning of the sentence. Then write each underlined word in the correct column.

ng 1. I had always wanted to see the singer named Amelia.

ch 2. My teacher said we would ride on a bus to see her.

th 3. I was third in line.

ck 4. I made sure I had my ticket.

ph 5. I wanted to get Amelia's autograph.

nk 6. I made sure my pen was full of ink.

sh 7. The show started when the clock struck noon.

gh 8. Amelia laughed as she walked on stage.

ch 9. The orchestra began to play.

wh 10. A white light filled the stage.

ch 11. Then Amelia and a choir of children began to sing.

tch 12. We'll watch Amelia again next year.

Beginning	Middle	End
_____	_____	_____
_____	_____	_____
_____	_____	_____
_____	_____	
_____		

82 Unit 3: Initial, Medial, and Final Consonant Digraphs

AT HOME Ask your child to make up sentences using five words that have a consonant digraph in the middle.

knot wrist comb light

Say each picture name. Circle the word that names the picture. Write the word.

RULE Sometimes consonants are **silent**. For example, the **k** in **knot** is silent. The words **wrist**, **comb**, and **light** also have silent consonants.

1. 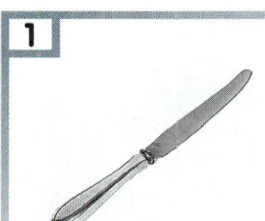 knife / night / knew

2.  wheat / wreath / wealth

3.  wrench / ranch / wreck

4.  fit / fight / filter

5.  lamb / lame / limb

6. 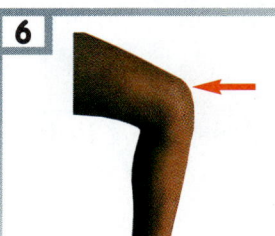 key / knee / kneel

7.  west / wrist / worst

8.  kite / knight / nickel

9. 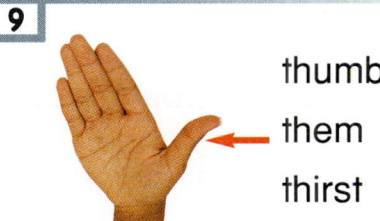 thumb / them / thirst

10. 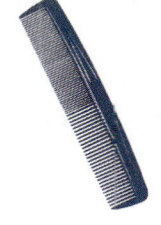 comb / come / column

11.  lit / light / like

12.  knob / nab / knock

Name _____

Unit 3: Silent Consonants

Find the two words in the wreath that have the same silent consonant or consonants as the first word. Write the words on the lines.

Words in the wreath: lamb, thumb, kneels, writer, wrap, night, light, knit

1. comb _____ _____
2. knob _____ _____
3. tight _____ _____
4. wrench _____ _____

Find the word in the wreath that completes each sentence. Write the word on the line.

5. I want to be a _____ when I grow up.

6. I write in my journal every _____ before I go to bed.

7. My mom tells me to turn off my _____ when it gets too late.

8. Sometimes I write so long that my _____ gets sore!

9. In my first story, a knight _____ before a king.

10. I also wrote a story about a _____ that gets lost from its flock.

11. My new story is about a a boy who can _____ magic hats.

12. I will _____ the story and give it to my mom.

Unit 3: Reading Words with Silent Consonants in Context

Ask your child to add one word to each group at the top of this page.

Read each clue and look at the picture. Use a word from the box to complete the answer. Write it on the line.

PHONICS and SPELLING

| clock | cough | frog | knob | match |
| phone | string | twelve | whale | wrist |

1
I am the biggest mammal.

I am a _____.

2
I live in a pond.

I am a _____.

3
I am a handle on a door.

I am a _____.

4
I am one dozen.

I am _____.

5
I will clear your throat.

I am a _____.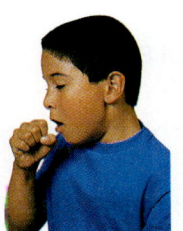

6
I have numbers and I ring.

I am a _____.

7
I have two hands and a face.

I am a _____.

8
I hold a kite.

I am a _____.

9
I can burn.

I am a _____.

10
I am the place for a watch.

I am a _____.

Name _____

Unit 3: Spelling Words with Consonant Blends and Digraphs and Silent Consonants

Circle the word that completes each sentence. Write the word on the line.

1. I dreamed of a beach that was pure and (clean, cheek). _____

2. There were white clouds in a blue (skip, sky). _____

3. (Chatter, Children) ran on the white sand. _____

4. I left my (shoes, choose) in the car and ran barefoot. _____

5. (Dolphins, Drops) swam near the shore. _____

6. A whale (sprayed, screened) water from its spout. _____

7. I picked up a (shell, steal) and put it in my pocket. _____

8. I (played, phoned) in the sand and made a castle. _____

9. I (wrist, wrote) a message in the sand. _____

10. It said, "(Thanks, Thinks) for this beautiful day!" _____

11. Even the seagulls (sang, sank) a special song. _____

12. It was a great day to (laugh, loud) and play. _____

13. At (knit, night), the sky was full of stars. _____

14. I hope that my dream comes (threw, true)! _____

Unit 3: Consonant Blends and Digraphs and Silent Consonants Review

Help your child draw a picture that includes all the details described on this page.

 Read the letter. Then read the sentences below it. Write the word that completes each sentence.

March 31, 2004

Dear Ling,

I hope that all of my friends will work together to feed the needy families in our town. I am writing to ask for your help with a special lunch.

On Thursday a dairy farmer gave cheese. Then a baker said she would give us her extra doughnuts. My sister got some fresh mushrooms from the farmers' market. My brother and his friends went to the beach and dug up some clams. I asked my mother to bake something. She agreed to make some wheat bread. On Friday I phoned three more people. A man with an orchard gave me twelve bushels of cherries. His friend gave me peach jam. I talked to the manager of our apartment building. She gave us chairs and tables to use for our lunch.

Can you help us, too? I hope so!

Your friend,
Chad

1. The dairy farmer gave _____ for the meal.

2. Chad's sister got _____ mushrooms from the market.

3. Chad's brother and his friends dug up _____ at the beach.

4. Chad's mother will bake _____ bread.

5. Chad used the _____ to call more friends.

6. The man with the orchard gave _____ bushels of cherries.

Name _____

Unit 3: Reading Words with Consonant Blends and Digraphs and Silent Consonants in Context

87

Write a letter to Chad. Tell him how you can help with his project. The words in the box may help you.

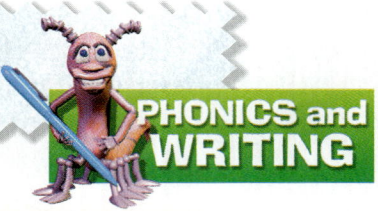

PHONICS and WRITING

| chicken | chips | lamb | might | radish | right |
| spinach | squash | thing | think | where | whole |

_____

_____,

_____
_____
_____
_____
_____
_____
_____
_____

_____,

_____

Unit 3: Writing Words with Consonant Blends and Digraphs and Silent Consonants

Write a letter to your child. Ask your child to write a letter back to you.

Say each picture name. Write the missing letters to complete the word.

Unit 3 CHECK-UP

1. ___unk
2. ___uit
3. ___ig
4. ___um
5. ba___
6. ___ale
7. ___eep
8. dol___in
9. lau___
10. chi___
11. ma___
12. ___ee
13. kni___t
14. ___ist
15. ___ake
16. ___ing
17. ___ow
18. te___
19. ___ef
20. thu___

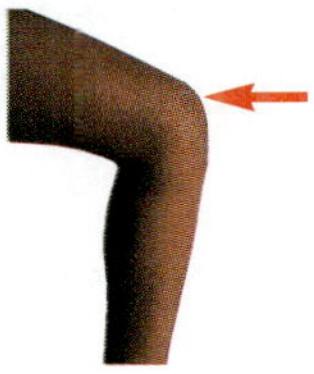

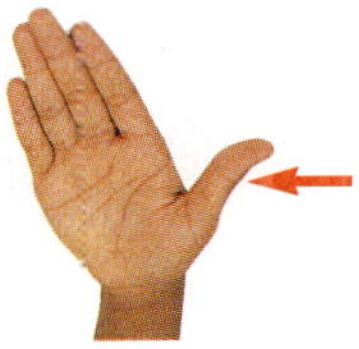

Name _____

Unit 3: Assessing Consonant Blends and Digraphs and Silent Consonants

89

Unit 3 CHECK-UP

Fill in the circle next to the word that completes each sentence.

1. I _____ about gardens growing everywhere.   ○ cream ○ dream ○ gleam ○ steam

2. Yellow _____ grows in office windows.   ○ wash ○ squish ○ squash ○ splash

3. A _____ tree grows in every front yard.   ○ peach ○ perch ○ pester ○ beach

4. Everybody has a green _____.   ○ them ○ thud ○ thug ○ thumb

5. Every empty lot is now a field of _____.   ○ cheat ○ wheat ○ whole ○ wheel

6. People greet each other with a _____.   ○ flower ○ flutter ○ farther ○ flounder

7. A _____ of flowers hangs on every door.   ○ wrench ○ wrist ○ wreck ○ wreath

8. Plants grow during all _____ months of the year.   ○ shelf ○ twist ○ twelve ○ shell

9. People don't spend a _____ on fruit or vegetables.   ○ cheek ○ tent ○ cent ○ sent

10. All the plants get plenty of water and _____.   ○ fright ○ flight ○ right ○ light

11. Berries and fruit trees grow by our _____.   ○ scream ○ stream ○ scram ○ scratch

12. I _____ it is a wonderful place.   ○ know ○ knit ○ knob ○ knock

Unit 3: Assessing Consonant Blends and Digraphs and Silent Consonants

UNIT 4
Around the World

r-Controlled Vowels, y as a Vowel, Vowel Digraphs, Diphthongs

Lunch Time

Oh, for a piece of papaya,
or a plate of beef lo mein—

Oh, for a bowl of Irish stew,
or fresh paella from Spain—

Oh, for a forkful of couscous,
or a chunk of Jarlsberg cheese—

Oh, for some lasagna,
or a bowl of black-eyed peas—

Of all the tasty foods
That I would love to try,

I sit here and wonder
why, oh why,
Mama packed me
this liverwurst on rye.

Lee Bennett Hopkins

Think About It

How does the speaker feel about liverwurst on rye? What are some more foods from other places?

Dear Family of _____,

Your child will be learning about *r*-controlled vowels, as in *farm* and *dirt*; *y* as a vowel, as in *cry* and *tiny*; vowel digraphs, as in *sleigh* and *stew*; and diphthongs, as in *how*, *toy*, and *coin*. Your child will be using these skills to read about the theme Around the World. Here are some activities you can do together.

- Help your child find a recipe for an international food dish. Read the ingredients and directions with your child. Together identify any words with *r*-controlled vowels, such as *corn, jar, stir, pear,* and *turkey*.

You might like to visit the library and find the book *The Chalk Doll* by Charlotte Pomerantz. Read it with your child.

- Imagine that you and your child are going to take a trip to Mexico or another warm-weather destination. Make a list of things you will take on your trip. Then have your child circle any vowel digraphs, such as the *ui* in *suit*, and underline any diphthongs, such as the *oy* in *toy* and the *ow* in *towel*.
- Give your child 60 seconds to write as many words as possible that contain *y* as a vowel, such as *sunny* and *my*. Help your child tell whether the *y* in each word has the long *i* sound or the long *e* sound.

Estimada familia de _____,

Su niño o niña aprenderá los sonidos en inglés de las vocales que vienen antes de la *r*, tales como en *farm* y *dirt*; la letra *y* como vocal, tal como en *cry* y *tiny*; dos vocales juntas que tienen un solo sonido, como en *sleigh* y *stew*; además de diptongos como en *how*, *toy* y *coin*. Su niño o niña usará estos conocimientos en su lectura sobre el tema de Alrededor del mundo (Around the World). Algunas actividades que usted y su niño o niña pueden hacer en inglés aparecen a continuación.

- Juntos busquen una receta para un plato de comida internacional. Lean los ingredientes y las instrucciones. Luego, identifiquen juntos cualquier palabra que tenga el sonido de una vocal antes de la letra *r*, tales como *corn, jar, pear* y *turkey*.
- Imagínense que ustedes van a irse de viaje a México o alguna otra parte de clima cálido. Juntos hagan una lista de lo que van a llevar de viaje. Luego, pida a su niño o niña que haga un círculo alrededor de cada palabra con vocales juntas que tengan un solo sonido, tales como ui en *suit* y que subraye todos los diptongos, tales como *oy* en *toy* y *ow* en *towel*.
- Dele a su niño o niña 60 segundos para escribir tantas palabras como sea posible que contengan la letra y como una vocal, tales como *sunny* y *my*. Ayude a su niño o niña a comentar si la letra y en cada palabra tiene el sonido "largo" de la *i* o el sonido "largo" de la *e*.

Unit 4: Family Involvement

car   corn   worm

The words at the left name the pictures in each row. Write each word under its picture. Then circle the letters in each word that stand for the vowel sound you hear in **car**, **corn**, or **worm**.

RULE When **r** follows a vowel, it changes the vowel sound. You can hear the **ar** sound in **car** and the **or** sounds in **corn** and **worm**. The vowel in each is neither long nor short.

fork
jar
porch
shark

1.  _____
2.  _____
3.  _____
4.  _____

star
horse
world
barn

5.  _____
6.  _____
7.  _____
8.  _____

Find the word in the box that completes each sentence. Write the word on the line.

dark
far
morning
north
world
worry
worth

9. People all around the _____ look at the stars.

10. We can see the stars best after _____.

11. By _____ the stars seem to disappear.

12. Just think how _____ away all those stars are!

13. Look _____, south, east, and west to see stars.

14. Don't _____ if you can't name many stars at first.

15. Learning about stars is _____ the effort.

Name _____

Unit 4: *r*-Controlled Vowels *ar* and *or*

93

fern **bird** **nurse**

Circle the word that names each picture. Write the word on the line.

RULE The letter pairs **er, ir,** and **ur** all have the same sound. You can hear this sound in **fern, bird,** and **nurse**. The vowel in each is neither short nor long.

1.    porch / purse / perch   _____

2.    square / squirted / squirrel   _____

3.    herd / hard / hurt   _____

4.    skirt / shirt / skill   _____

5.    crab / curb / crib   _____

6.    paper / person / purple   _____

7.    cinch / circle / curdle   _____

8.    turned / thirteen / turtle   _____

9.    twirl / twig / twelve   _____

Find the word in the box that completes each sentence. Write the word on the line.

| burning |
| certain |
| circus |
| girl |
| turn |

10. The _____ had animals from around the world.

11. We saw ten tiny dogs _____ flips in the air.

12. Three tigers jumped through _____ hoops of fire.

13. A _____ danced on the back of a prancing horse.

14. I am _____ that I don't want to try that trick!

Unit 4: *r*-Controlled Vowels *er, ir,* and *ur*

Ask your child to think of more words with the *er, ir,* and *ur* vowel sound. Have your child use the words in sentences.

94

 chair 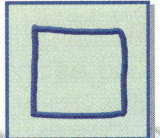 square  bear

RULE The letters **air, are,** and **ear** can stand for the same sound. You can hear this sound in **chair, square,** and **bear**.

Say each picture name. If the word has the same vowel sound that you hear in **chair, square,** and **bear,** write the letters to complete the word.

1. __h__air
2. __b__ear__d__
3. __m__are
4. __d__art__s__
5. __p__ear
6. __st__air__s__
7. __b__are
8. __h__ear__t__
9. __p__air

Find the word in the box that completes each sentence. Write the word on the line.

fairs
hair
pears
share
tear
wear

10. People all over the world have fun at _____.

11. Farmers come to sell _____ and other fruits.

12. Some people _____ their foods and crafts.

13. Dancers often _____ colorful costumes.

14. Sometimes the dancers put flowers in their _____.

15. They must be careful not to _____ their fancy clothes!

Name _____

beard   cheer   Earth

Read each sentence. Circle each word that contains the vowel sound you hear in **beard** and **cheer** or **Earth**. Then write the words you circled in the correct column below.

RULE The letters **ear** and **eer** can stand for the vowel sound you hear in **beard** and **cheer**.
   The letters **ear** can also stand for the vowel sound you hear in **Earth**.

1. All over the world, many people live in or near cities.
2. They peer out their windows at the city streets.
3. Other people live on farms where they plow the earth.
4. They rise early when they hear the rooster crow.
5. It is hard to earn a living far from a city or a farm.
6. Most people search hard for a good job.
7. Some people must learn new skills for a job.
8. A job that you have for many years is called a career.

ear as in **beard**   **eer** as in **cheer**   **ear** as in **Earth**

_____   _____   _____

_____   _____   _____

_____   _____

        _____

        _____

Unit 4: *r*-Controlled Vowels *ear* and *eer*

Help your child to think of other words that have the same vowel sounds as those in *beard, cheer,* and *Earth.*

**Circle the word that completes each sentence.
Write the word on the line.**

1. Nora and her family will never _____ their trip to Ireland.
   forest   forget   furrow

2. They got up _____ one morning to visit Galway Bay.
   early   earnest   eagle

3. They drove through the chilly _____ and clouds of fog.
   ape   art   air

4. It was hard to _____ through the fog.
   pear   peer   pair

5. Then the fog lifted and they got a _____ view of the bay.
   clear   cheer   chorus

6. "Ireland is the most beautiful place in the _____!" shouted Nora.
   world   work   worth

7. Then Nora's family visited an Irish _____.
   form   firm   farm

8. Nora's brother _____ her to pet a sheep.
   dreary   dared   darken

9. The farmer let her touch its _____ wool.
   cured   curb   curly

10. Nora's family bought wool sweaters to _____ home.
    wear   wore   were

Name _____

Unit 4: Reading Words with *r*-Controlled Vowels in Context

Make a word by drawing a line from a syllable in the first column to a syllable in the second column. Then write the word on the line.

RULE A **syllable** is a word or a word part with one vowel sound. **Rug** has one syllable, **cabin** has two syllables, and **umbrella** has three syllables.

1. sur   cus   _____
2. cir   ple   _____
3. bor   der   _____
4. pur   prise _____

5. birth get   _____
6. bar   day   _____
7. har   ber   _____
8. for   bor   _____

Write the word from the box that completes each sentence. Then write the number of syllables in the word.

| bargain | clear | ears | fair |
| gardens | grocery | harvest | Saturday |

9. Many farmers grow vegetables in big _____. ___

10. Some farmers sell their _____ at a farmers' market. ___

11. A farmers' market is like a county _____. ___

12. _____ is a favorite day to hold a farmers' market. ___

13. The market is a good place to buy beans, peas, and _____ of corn. ___

14. Most people buy their food at a big _____ store. ___

15. These stores can sell food at _____ prices. ___

16. But it is _____ that many people like to shop at a farmers' market. ___

Unit 4: Syllables in Words with *r*-Controlled Vowels

Have your child point out words with two or more syllables in the sentences above.

 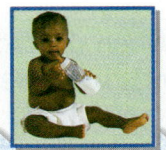 

fly   baby   gym

RULE The letter **y** can act as a vowel. You can hear the **long i** sound of **y** in **fly**, the **long e** sound of **y** in **baby**, and the **short i** sound of **y** in **gym**.

Find the word in the box that names each picture. Write the word on the line. Then write the word in the correct column below.

bicycle	cherry	cry
cymbals	fry	funny
penny	pyramid	sky

1.  _____
2.  _____
3.  _____
4. 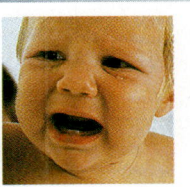 _____
5.  _____
6.  _____
7.  _____
8.  _____
9.  _____

y as long i   **y as long e**   **y as short i**

Name _____

Unit 4: **y** as a Vowel

Say each word in the box. Write the word in the correct column below.

RULES When a word with one syllable ends in **y**, the **y** usually has the **long i** sound.

When a word with two or more syllables ends in **y**, the **y** usually has the **long e** sound.

When **y** comes in the middle of a word or a syllable, it usually has the **short i** sound.

cry	fly	history
mystery	rainy	shy
sunny	syllable	system

One Syllable **Two Syllables** **Three Syllables**

_____ _____ _____

_____ _____ _____

_____ _____ _____

Say each word below. Write the number of syllables you hear on the line. Then use the words to complete the sentences.

| city ____ | dry ____ | Egypt ____ | mystery ____ |
| pyramid ____ | royalty ____ | symbols ____ | why ____ |

1. A _____ is a large building with sides shaped like triangles.

2. Many were built long ago in the country of _____.

3. You can find them there in the hot, _____ desert.

4. Experts know _____ they were built.

5. They were built as a place to bury kings and other _____.

6. Most are as tall as the skyscrapers in a _____.

7. Some have strange signs and _____ carved on them.

8. How they were built is still a _____.

Point to some words on the page with the letter **y**. Ask your child to identify the vowel sound that the letter **y** stands for.

Unit 4: Syllables in Words with **y** as a Vowel

Use the code to write each missing word.

1 = a	2 = b	3 = c	4 = d	5 = e	6 = h
7 = i	8 = l	9 = m	10 = n	11 = o	12 = p
13 = r	14 = s	15 = t	16 = w	17 = y	

1. Sailors long ago traveled all over the __ __ __ __ __ .
   16 11 13 8 4

2. Some sailors told stories about __ __ __ __ __ __ __ __ .
   9 5 13 9 1 7 4 14

3. Most sailors were not __ __ __ about telling their stories.
   14 6 17

4. Some sailors dove to __ __ __ __ __ __ for __ __ __ __ __ __ __ .
   14 5 1 13 3 6   12 5 1 13 8 14

5. A __ __ __ __ __ __ __ __ __ __ __ could send a sailor's
   16 7 10 4 17 14 15 11 13 9

   ship off course.

6. The wind could __ __ __ __ a ship's sails.
   15 5 1 13

7. Many ships were lost every __ __ __ __ .
   17 5 1 13

8. A lighthouse helped during the __ __ __ __ __ storms.
   16 11 13 14 15

9. The lighthouse keeper had many __ __ __ __ __ __
   14 15 1 7 13 14

   to climb.

10. The __ __ __ __ __ of a foghorn helped, too.
    2 8 1 13 5

Name _____

Unit 4: Spelling Words with *r*-Controlled Vowels and *y* as a Vowel

Find the word in the box that matches each clue. Then write the word in the crossword puzzle.

air
darkness
gardens
germs
girl
gym
lark
pearl
rare
scary
sky
star
steer
store
year

Across
1. places filled with flowers
4. a singing bird
6. not common
7. a sun
9. to guide
10. twelve months
11. tiny things that can make you sick

Down
1. a young female person
2. the opposite of *lightness*
3. a place to buy things
5. what we breathe
7. frightening
8. a white jewel
11. a place to play sports
12. where you'll find stars and planets

Unit 4: *r*-Controlled Vowels and *y* as a Vowel Review

Ask your child to think of words that rhyme with some of the answers in the word box.

Read the story. Then read the sentences below it. Write the word that completes each sentence.

Mount Everest

Mount Everest is the highest mountain on Earth. It is more than 29,000 feet tall. It is in the mountain range called the Himalayas. People who live in this mountain range call it the Roof of the World.

Mountain climbers first reached the top of Mount Everest in 1953. Only two people made it to the top that year. In later years thousands climbed to the top. Many of them left their garbage behind. The Roof of the World was littered with tons of garbage. The problem became an emergency.

In 1994 five American climbers went up the mountain. They brought back more than 5,000 pounds of ripped-up tents and camping gear, batteries, and other garbage. They also paid Sherpas to carry garbage down Mount Everest. The Sherpas are the people who live near the mountain.

Today cleanup crews search for the worst dumps. They hope that future climbers will carry their own garbage down the mountain. They want the Roof of the World to be clean again.

1. Mount Everest is _____ than 29,000 feet tall.

2. People first stood at the top of Mount Everest in the _____ 1953.

3. Many climbers left old tents and other _____ on the mountain.

4. The garbage problem became an _____.

5. The _____ live near Mount Everest.

6. Cleanup crews try to find the _____ dumps.

Name _____

Unit 4: Reading Words with *r*-Controlled Vowels and *y* as a Vowel in Context

What can you do to keep Earth clean? Write a paragraph telling ways to keep our planet clean and healthy. The words in the box may help you.

bicycle	pretty
burning	recycle
clear	search
dark	share
Earth	sky
farm	system
forest	world
garbage	

 bread
 sleigh

Say each picture name. Write **ea** or **ei** on the line to complete the word.

RULE A **vowel digraph** is two vowels that are together. Vowel digraphs can have a short vowel sound, a long vowel sound, or a sound all their own.

The vowel digraph **ea** can stand for the **short e** sound you hear in **bread**.

The vowel digraph **ei** can stand for the **long a** sound you hear in **sleigh**.

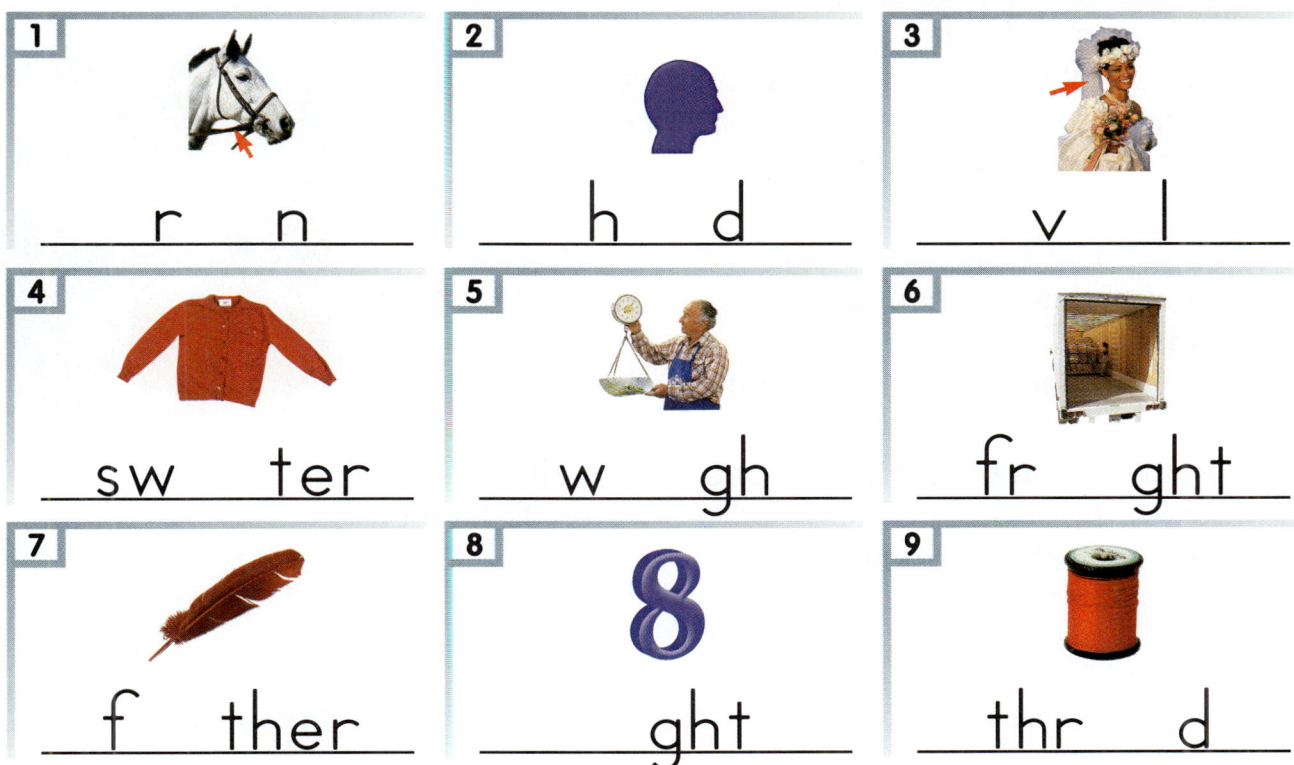

1. __r__n
2. __h__d
3. __v__l
4. sw__ter
5. __w__gh
6. fr__ght
7. __f__ther
8. __ght
9. thr__d

Find the word in the box that completes each sentence. Write the word on the line.

breath
freight
instead
neighbor
ready
weather

10. Canada is a _____ of the United States.

11. We are _____ for a great day.

12. We watch the _____ train pass.

13. The _____ is perfect for a picnic.

14. I want ketchup _____ of mustard.

15. I will be out of _____ if I run up that hill.

Name _____

Unit 4: Vowel Digraphs *ea* and *ei*

Read the story. Underline each word that has the **short e** sound of **ea**. Circle each word that has the **long a** sound of **ei**. Then circle and write the word that completes each sentence.

Emma and her neighbor, Hans, live in Germany. After breakfast one day, they rode horses in the hills outside Munich. Emma's horse didn't like the weight of the saddle on its back.

"That saddle is very heavy," Hans said.

Emma held the leather reins and patted the horse gently. They rode until they saw a meadow on the hillside ahead.

"This is heavenly," said Hans. "Look at all these flowers. Daisies and heather are spread out as far as I can see."

"The weather is nice, too," Emma said. She slid off her horse and tied her sweater around her waist.

Emma's horse neighed once and lowered its head. It began to eat the grass. They were all ready to take a pleasant break from riding.

1. Emma and Hans are _____.
   reindeer   neighbors   treasures

2. Emma's horse had a _____ saddle.
   sweaty   heavy   eighty

3. The horse didn't like the _____ of the saddle.
   weight   eighteen   vein

4. Emma and Hans stopped in a _____ full of flowers.
   breakfast   measure   meadow

5. There were daisies and _____ on the hillside.
   heaven   heather   sweater

6. The _____ was nice and warm.
   weather   feather   freight

Unit 4: Vowel Digraphs *ea* and *ei*

Ask your child to add a sentence to the story using a word with *ea* or *ei*.

 book  moon

RULE The vowel digraph **oo** can stand for the vowel sounds you hear in **book** and **moon**.

Circle the word that names each picture. Write the word on the line.

1.  would / wood / word _____

2.  roof / ruff / root _____

3.  hoop / honk / hook _____

4.  wool / work / wall _____

5.  racing / racket / raccoon _____

6. school / scold / should _____

Circle the word that completes each sentence. Write the word on the line.

7. A _____ has animals from many parts of the world.   zoom   zoo   soot

8. The _____ is a monkey that lives in Africa.   book   bone   baboon

9. The _____ is a large mammal from Australia.   kangaroo   kettle   kitchen

10. The penguins swim in their own special _____.   spool   pole   pool

11. It's fun to _____ at all the different creatures.   look   lock   loom

12. My mom always buys me a big red _____ before we leave!   broom   brook   balloon

Name _____

Unit 4: Vowel Digraph *oo*

Read the story. Circle each word that has the oo digraph. Write each word in the correct column below.

The Paynes raise sheep in New Zealand. Wool is an important product in their country. The Paynes didn't learn their skills in school. It took a long time to learn how to raise the best sheep.

The Paynes look over their flock carefully. They feed the sheep the best food and check their health often. They guide the sheep to pasture with big canes made of bamboo.

One cool spring night, Nate Payne was in his room. He heard a ewe, a female sheep, crying. Nate stood up and put on his boots. He went out to find the ewe. He saw her standing in the moonlight. She was caught in a hawthorn bush. Her foot was stuck in the woody branches. Her curly hair was tangled in the thorns.

"Goodness!" Nate said as he knelt down to help her. "You have really cooked your goose!" He carefully unhooked the thorns from the ewe's thick fur.

oo as in book

_____ _____

_____ _____

_____ _____

_____ _____

_____

oo as in moon

_____ _____

_____ _____

_____ _____

_____ _____

Ask your child to make a list of animals whose names have the **oo** digraph.

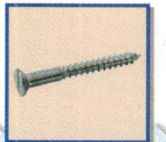 screw  fruit

Circle the word that names each picture. Write the word on the line.

RULE The vowel digraphs **ew** and **ui** can stand for the same vowel sound. You can hear this vowel sound in **screw** and **fruit**.

1. jester / jewel / jelly
2. suit / soup / soon
3. needle / newspaper / noontime
4. stem / straw / stew
5. chew / choose / cherry
6. junk / judge / juice

Find the word in the box that completes each sentence. Write the word on the line.

blew
crew
cruise
few
flew
fruit
juicy
new

7. The Chen family went on a _____ to the South Pacific.

8. The ship was _____ and had never sailed before.

9. The ship's _____ gave the Chens flowers.

10. The Chens visited quite a _____ beautiful islands.

11. A soft warm breeze _____ through the tall palm trees.

12. Colorful birds _____ all around and perched nearby.

13. Mrs. Chen fed them little pieces of _____.

14. The birds loved the _____ treat!

Name _____

Unit 4: Vowel Digraphs *ew* and *ui*   109

Circle the word that completes each sentence. Write the word on the line.

1. Maria reads the paper every day to keep up with the _____. nose news noose

2. Yesterday Maria read about a frost that hurt the _____ trees in Florida. foot fruit friend

3. The morning _____ froze on the plants. due dew do

4. Some oranges were _____ when they fell to the ground. brushed bruised brood

5. Maria thinks that the price of _____ will go up soon. juice joyous jelly

6. Then Maria read about a famous artist that her mother _____. knee kneel knew

7. The artist sailed around the world to find the best _____. vow view vowel

8. She _____ pictures of the places she liked most. drew drain dregs

9. She painted sea gulls that _____ over England's cliffs. flea few flew

10. She painted the ocean as the wind _____ over the waves. blue blew blend

11. She even sketched the ship's cook as he made a _____. strew stood stew

12. She had many works of art at the end of her _____! cruise crews crows

Unit 4: Vowel Digraphs *ew* and *ui*

Read a newspaper with your child and look for words with *ew* or *ui*.

 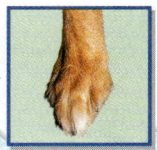  

haul paw chalk ball

Say each picture name. Write **au**, **aw**, or **al** on the line to complete the word.

RULES The vowel digraphs **au** and **aw** can stand for the same vowel sound. You can hear this vowel sound in **haul** and **paw**.

The letters **al** can stand for this same vowel sound. You can hear this sound in **chalk** and **ball**.

1. f__all__l
2. y__aw__n
3. w__al__k
4. v__au__lt
5. s__aw__
6. f__au__cet
7. l__aw__n
8. w__al__l
9. s__au__cer
10. cr__aw__l
11. astron__au__t
12. h__aw__k

Name _____

Unit 4: *au*, *aw*, and *al*

Find the word in the box that completes each sentence. Write the word on the line.

always	autumn	bald	baseball	call
crawl	dawn	launch	salty	sauce
saw	shawl	smallest	talk	tall

1. I have _____ liked to learn about other places.
2. My grandmother bought a beautiful knitted _____ in Russia.
3. My uncle learned to make spicy tomato _____ in Italy.
4. When it is _____ in South America, it is spring in Canada.
5. The _____ eagle is the national bird of the United States.
6. The hummingbird is one of the _____ birds in the world.
7. When the sun sets in Brazil, it is _____ in Australia.
8. Ramon knows how to _____ in sign language.
9. The Great Salt Lake in Utah has _____ water.
10. I watched a rocket _____ in Florida.
11. I wonder how much a phone _____ to Spain costs.
12. All kinds of insects fly and _____ through the rain forest.
13. My mom went to Paris and _____ the Eiffel Tower.
14. It is a very _____ landmark.
15. A popular sport in Japan is _____.

 Unit 4: *au*, *aw*, and *al*

 Point to words in the box and have your child think of three rhyming words for each word that you point out.

cough   couple   four   soup

Say each word in the box. Then write the word in the correct column below.

RULE The vowel digraph **ou** can stand for several different vowel sounds. You can hear these different sounds in **cough, couple, four,** and **soup**.

bought	cougar	course	cousin	double	fought
group	ought	pour	rough	source	thought
through	trouble	your	youth		

ou in **cough**   **ou** in **couple**   **ou** in **four**   **ou** in **soup**

_____   _____   _____   _____

_____   _____   _____   _____

_____   _____   _____   _____

_____   _____   _____   _____

Find the word in the box that completes each sentence. Write the word on the line.

brought
countries
enough
gourds
tough
you

1. The Pilgrims came to New England from _____ in Europe.

2. They had a _____ time settling in America.

3. The Native Americans _____ food to help them through the winter.

4. The Pilgrims learned how to grow pumpkins and _____.

5. Soon there was _____ food to keep the pilgrims alive.

6. Would _____ be helpful to a new friend?

Name _____

Unit 4: **ou** as a Vowel Digraph

mouse

Say each picture name. If the word has the same vowel sound that you hear in **mouse**, write the diphthong **ou** to complete the word.

RULE A **diphthong** is two vowels blended together to make one vowel sound. The diphthong **ou** can stand for the vowel sound you hear in **mouse**.

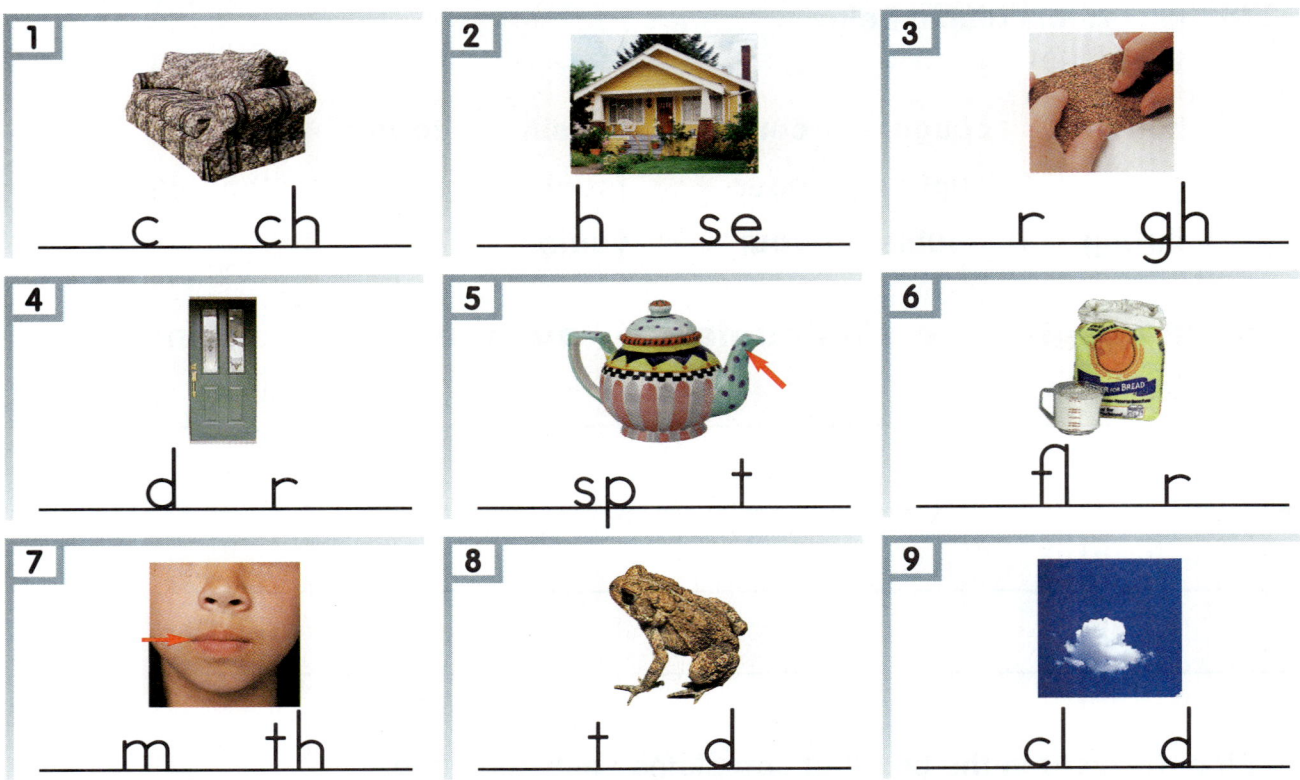

1. c __ou__ ch
2. h __ou__ se
3. r __ou__ gh
4. d __oo__ r
5. sp __ou__ t
6. fl __ou__ r
7. m __ou__ th
8. t __oa__ d
9. cl __ou__ d

Circle the word that completes each sentence. Write the word on the line.

10. My _____ troop went camping in the Rockies.   scout   shout   scoot

11. We hiked high into the _____.   mouse   monthly   mountains

12. We _____ a shady spot to camp.   found   fund   fought

13. It was fun to sleep on the _____!   group   ground   grouch

14. Then we went fishing for _____.   tough   trout   through

15. We caught more fish than we could _____.   cough   count   country

Unit 4: *ou* as a Diphthong

Ask your child to tell you a story using some of the picture names.

cow   crow

Circle the word that names each picture. Write the word on the line.

RULE The diphthong **ow** can stand for the sound you hear in **cow**. It can also stand for the **long o** sound you hear in **crow**.

1.
   - snore
   - snoop
   - snow

2.
   - owl
   - old
   - ouch

3.
   - blouse
   - blow
   - blond

4.
   - crawl
   - crown
   - crew

5.
   - ball
   - bow
   - bowl

6.
   - flowed
   - flour
   - flower

Find the word in the box that completes each sentence. Write the word on the line. Then circle the word if it has the same vowel sound as cow.

arrows   bow   down   grow   tower   window

7. The crown jewels of England are in a _____ in London.

8. It is an adventure to sail _____ the Amazon River.

9. In the sport of archery, people use bows and _____.

10. A _____ is a polite greeting in Japan.

11. Most plants won't _____ in the Sahara Desert.

12. What can you see out your _____?

Name _____

Unit 4: Sounds of *ow*   115

boy   coins

The words at the left name the pictures in each row. Write each word under its picture.

RULE The diphthongs **oy** and **oi** stand for the same vowel sound. You can hear this sound in **boy** and **coins**.

toys
soil
point

1.  _____
2.  _____
3.  _____

coil
broil
noise

4.  _____
5.  _____
6.  _____

boil
oyster
foil

7.  _____
8.  _____
9.  _____

Find the word in the box that completes each sentence. Write the word on the line.

annoy
enjoy
join
oil
voyage

10. Would you _____ exploring the South Pole?

11. It is not easy to _____ a team of explorers.

12. You would have to be strong enough for the _____.

13. Explorers once used _____ lanterns.

14. Good explorers do not let the cold weather _____ them.

Have your child find Antarctica on a map of the world. Then have your child write a sentence about a voyage to the South Pole.

Unit 4: Diphthongs *oy* and *oi*

PHONICS and SPELLING

Read each sentence. Replace **suitcase** with the correct word from the box. Write the word on the line at the bottom of the page.

1. Have you ever **suitcase** about living in another country?
2. In Peru you could watch **suitcase** fly high in the sky.
3. In Italy cooks add tomato **suitcase** to many foods.
4. You would need big scales to **suitcase** an Indian elephant.
5. You can see rain **suitcase** down in the rain forest.
6. Would you like to fish in a **suitcase** in Sweden?
7. The howler monkeys in South America are **suitcase**.
8. This **suitcase** came from a mine in South Africa.
9. Pineapple is a **suitcase** fruit from Hawaii.
10. How about a **suitcase** scoop of French vanilla ice cream?
11. My Chinese doll wears a red silk **suitcase**.
12. My family went to Mexico with a **suitcase** of friends.
13. Are you packed and **suitcase** to take a trip?
14. I like to travel **suitcase** the world.
15. But I am **suitcase** every time I come home.
16. Home is **suitcase** the best place to be.

| always |
| around |
| brook |
| double |
| gown |
| group |
| hawks |
| jewel |
| joyful |
| juicy |
| noisy |
| pour |
| ready |
| sauce |
| thought |
| weigh |

1. _____ 2. _____ 3. _____
4. _____ 5. _____ 6. _____
7. _____ 8. _____ 9. _____
10. _____ 11. _____ 12. _____
13. _____ 14. _____ 15. _____
16. _____

Name _____

Unit 4: Spelling Words with Vowel Digraphs and Diphthongs

Find and circle the words from the box in the puzzle below. The words can go across or down.

```
v a u l t m a l l x
o a w e s p o o n n
w j o y a l l c e e
b e c a u s e n i w
o w r w c p a o g s
u e e n e r a i h p
n l w k a e n s b a
d t o u r a n e o p
b o o k t d o a r e
t o u g h k y o u r
```

all
annoy
awe
book
bound
cause
crew
earth
jewel
joy
mall
neighbor
newspaper
noise
sauce
spoon
spread
too
tough
tour
vault
vow
yawn
your

Find the word in the box that completes each sentence. Write the word on the line.

1. Another word for *dirt* is _____.

2. A diamond or a ruby is a _____.

3. You feel _____ if you feel great happiness.

4. A _____ is something you use to eat soup.

5. Money in a bank is kept in a _____.

6. A _____ is a shopping center.

7. Meat that is hard to chew is _____.

8. The person who lives next to you is your _____.

9. You might _____ if you are very tired.

Unit 4: Vowel Digraphs and Diphthongs Review

Ask your child to explain what some of the other words in the box mean.

Read the story. Then read the sentences below it. Write the word that completes each sentence.

A Koi Story

Some fish farmers in Japan raise large goldfish called koi. These fish come in many colors. People like to watch koi swim around. Watching them helps people feel calm and relaxed.

A boy named Yuji talked his parents into getting a few koi. They bought four fish and put them in a pond near the house. They throw coins into the pool and make wishes. They feed the koi special food. The fish seem to enjoy their new home well enough. Now there are fourteen of them.

One day Yuji was playing baseball in the yard with a couple of friends. Just as he threw the ball, he tripped over a coil of hose. The ball went into the pond. Most of the koi swam down and away, but one jumped out of the pool.

"Quick!" Yuji shouted loudly. "Throw it back in! It can't breathe air!"

His friend Toshi picked up the fish and lowered it into the water. It didn't move. It looked more brown than gold. "I'm sorry," Toshi said with a frown.

Suddenly the koi leaped off Toshi's hands and swam away. "Good!" said Toshi. "It's not dead. I guess it's all better now."

1. Yuji and his family have large goldfish called _____.

2. Watching the fish swim _____ can make people feel calm.

3. Yuji's family _____ four of the large goldfish.

4. A _____ fell into the fish pond.

5. Toshi thought the fish was _____ until it swam away.

Name _____

Reading Words with Vowel Digraphs and Diphthongs in Context

Pretend you could have a pet from another part of the world. Write a paragraph about the animal you would like to have. Describe the animal and tell why it would make a good pet. The words in the box may help you.

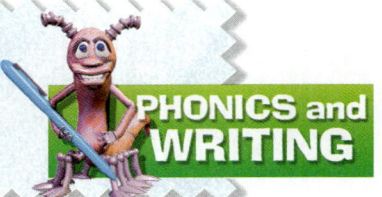

PHONICS and WRITING

bowl	brown	crawl	enjoy	feather
food	flew	grow	noise	owl
ought	reindeer	trouble	walk	wool

_____
_____
_____
_____
_____
_____
_____
_____

Unit 4: Writing Words with Vowel Digraphs and Diphthongs

AT HOME Ask your child to read the paragraph to you.

Circle the word that names each picture. Write the word on the line.

Unit 4 CHECK-UP

1.  warm / worm / word / work
2.  cool / cold / coil / color
3.  turtle / turkey / turned / total
4.  old / ouch / off / owl
5.  stores / stares / stairs / stirs
6.  wood / wool / wheel / would
7.  laws / lawn / loan / long
8.  dear / deer / dreary / drag
9.  shout / sport / spout / sprout
10.  star / stall / start / storm
11.  spool / stool / screw / school
12.  eight / eighty / earth / weight
13.  sty / spy / sky / say
14.  strew / stem / step / stew
15.  heed / head / heard / hard

Name _____

Unit 4: Assessing *r*-Controlled Vowels, *y* as a Vowel, Vowel Digraphs, and Diphthongs

Fill in the circle next to the word that best completes each sentence.

1. One day I will take a _____ around the world.
   - ○ volcano
   - ○ vowel
   - ○ voices
   - ○ voyage

2. The rain _____ is home to many important plants and animals.
   - ○ fourteen
   - ○ forest
   - ○ forty
   - ○ force

3. My teacher went to Tanzania and saw a _____ of zebra.
   - ○ horse
   - ○ herd
   - ○ heard
   - ○ hurt

4. There are _____ on every continent on Earth.
   - ○ moving
   - ○ mouthy
   - ○ mother
   - ○ mountains

5. Lets play a game where we stand in a _____.
   - ○ syllable
   - ○ circle
   - ○ cymbal
   - ○ cyclone

6. I like to _____ downtown in the cities I visit.
   - ○ wail
   - ○ wall
   - ○ wake
   - ○ walk

7. The _____ in Egypt were built as tombs for kings.
   - ○ parachutes
   - ○ pretty
   - ○ pyramids
   - ○ pygmies

8. Would you like to take a _____ to Greece?
   - ○ crowds
   - ○ crews
   - ○ cruise
   - ○ clues

9. Don't be _____ to try new things.
   - ○ scarf
   - ○ scared
   - ○ scratched
   - ○ scarred

10. You have to get up _____ to watch the sunrise.
    - ○ earning
    - ○ every
    - ○ early
    - ○ earthy

Unit 4: Assessing *r*-Controlled Vowels, *y* as a Vowel, Vowel Digraphs, and Diphthongs

UNIT 5
Helping Out

Compound Words, Schwa, Inflectional Endings, Syllables, Plurals, Contractions, Possessives

Jim

There never was a nicer boy
Than Mrs. Jackson's Jim.
The sun should drop its greatest gold
On him.

Because, when Mother-dear was sick,
He brought her cocoa in.
And brought her broth, and brought her bread.
And brought her medicine.

And, tipping, tidied up her room.
And would not let her see
He missed his game of baseball
Terribly.

— Gwendolyn Brooks

Think About It

Why didn't Jim let his mother know how much he missed his baseball game?
What things do you do to help others?

Dear Family of _____,

Your child will be learning about compound words, the schwa sound, inflectional endings, syllables, plurals, contractions, and possessives. You child will be using these skills to read about the theme Helping Out. Here are some activities you can do together.

- Take a walk around the house with your child. Have your child write sentences using singular and plural possessives to identify belongings, such as *This is Mom's briefcase* and *The dogs' toys are outside*.
- Have your child make a chart of the chores he or she does at home. Read together the list of chores on the chart. Have your child clap the number of syllables in each word after you read it. Display the chart on your refrigerator.

LIBRARY LINK

You might like to visit the library and find the book *The Rescue of Brown Bear and White Bear* by Martine Beck. Read it with your child.

- Play Contraction Concentration. Make two sets of cards, one that shows the two words that form a contraction, such as *have not*, and the other set that shows the actual contractions, such as *haven't*. Shuffle the cards and place each face down on a table. Take turns trying to turn over a matching pair of cards.

Estimada familia de _____,

Su niño o niña aprenderá palabras compuestas en inglés, el sonido de la *schwa*, afijos, sílabas, el plural de las palabras, contracciones y posesivos. Él o ella usará estos conocimientos en su lectura sobre el tema Ayudar (Helping Out). Algunas actividades que usted y su niño o niña pueden hacer en inglés aparecen a continuación.

- Juntos recorran la casa y pídale a su niño o niña que escriba oraciones que tengan el posesivo en singular y plural en inglés para identificar artículos, tales como "*This is Mom's briefcase*" y "*The dogs' toys are outside*".
- Invite a su niño o niña a que haga una gráfica que muestre las tareas que él o ella hace en la casa. Juntos lean la lista de tareas de la gráfica. Pídale a su niño o niña que después de cada palabra que usted lea, dé una palmada por cada sílaba que tenga cada palabra. Despliegue la gráfica en su refrigerador.
- Jueguen a "concentración en la contracción". Hagan dos conjuntos de tarjetas, uno que muestre las dos palabras que forman una contracción, tales como *have not* y el otro conjunto que muestre la contracción ya formada, tales como *haven't*. Baraje las tarjetas y póngalas boca abajo en la mesa. Túrnense tratando de volver boca arriba un par de tarjetas que correspondan.

Chores
Dry dishes
Set table
Clean bedroom
Walk dog

Read the two words that make up each picture name. Then write the compound word.

RULE A **compound word** is two words joined together to make one word. **Seashore** is a compound word made by joining the words **sea** and **shore**.

1.
fire + place
_____

2.
bird + house
_____

3.
row + boat
_____

4.
news + paper
_____

5.
paint + brush
_____

6.
basket + ball
_____

Write the two words that make up each compound word.

7. baseball _____ _____

8. seashell _____ _____

9. popcorn _____ _____

10. bathtub _____ _____

11. flashlight _____ _____

12. homework _____ _____

13. upstairs _____ _____

Name _____

Unit 5: Compound Words

Write the compound word that completes each sentence.

1. A _____ is a ball that you kick with your foot.
2. A _____ is a coat that you wear in the rain.
3. A _____ is a board where a score is kept.
4. A _____ is a ship that travels into space.
5. A _____ is a bird that has blue feathers.
6. A _____ is a house built in a tree.
7. A _____ is a boat that has a sail.
8. A _____ is a pot that you use to make tea.

Circle the compound word in each sentence. Then write the two words that make up the compound word.

9. Alex helped Alan build a doghouse for his puppy. _____ _____

10. He measured the wood with a yardstick. _____ _____

11. Dana brought me my homework when I was sick. _____ _____

12. He brought my notebook and my pen. _____ _____

13. Barbara keeps the lunchroom clean. _____ _____

14. Bill sweeps the dirt into a dustpan. _____ _____

15. Will you help me bake a birthday cake for Ben? _____ _____

Unit 5: Compound Words

Ask your child to think of compound words that contain *book, house, light,* and *sea*.

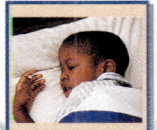    

asleep　　melon　　pencil　　circus　　elephant

The words at the left name the pictures in each row. Write each word under its picture. Then circle the vowel that stands for the schwa sound.

RULE The **schwa** is the vowel sound you hear in an unstressed syllable. Any vowel can stand for the schwa sound. You can hear the schwa sound in **asleep, melon, pencil, circus,** and **elephant**.

seven
walrus
zebra

1.
_____
2. _____
3. _____

gerbil
wagon
telephone

4.
_____
5.
_____
6.
_____

Write each word from the box in the correct column below.

| adult | apricot | cactus | camel | canoe |
| children | circus | family | parrot | ribbon |

Schwa Spelled a　　**Schwa Spelled o**　　**Schwa Spelled i**

_____　　_____　　_____

_____　　_____　　_____

Schwa Spelled u　　**Schwa Spelled e**

_____　　_____

_____　　_____

Name _____

Unit 5: Schwa

Find the word in the box that completes each sentence. Write the word on the line.

album	alone	carrots	eleven
fossils	lemons	possible	presents
problems	science	shovel	walrus

1. Cyrus only has _____ cents in his bank.

2. He wants to give his family some _____.

3. Cyrus knows that it is _____ to give presents that don't cost money.

4. He can help his sister study for her _____ test.

5. Cyrus can help his brother solve his math _____.

6. Cyrus can squeeze _____ to make his dad's favorite drink.

7. He can help his uncle hunt for _____.

8. Next winter he can help _____ the snow.

9. Cyrus can paint a picture of a _____ or a whale for his aunt.

10. Cyrus can help his mom peel _____ and potatoes for dinner.

11. He can visit his grandmother, who lives all _____.

12. Cyrus can make a photo _____ for his family.

Help your child make a list of presents that do not cost money. Have your child point out any words with the **schwa** sound.

Read each base word below. Add the ending to the base word. Write the new word on the line.

> **RULES** An **ending** is a word part added at the end of a word. The word to which an ending is added is called a **base word**. **S, es, ed,** and **ing** are endings.
> - If a base word ends in **ch, s, sh, ss, x,** or **z**, add **es**. Otherwise, add **s**.
>   brush   brush**es**   pull   pull**s**
> - Adding an ending can change the spelling of the base word.
>   study   stud**ies**   stud**ied**
>   wag   wag**ged**   wag**ging**
>   hike   hik**ed**   hik**ing**

1. run + ing = _____
2. guess + es = _____
3. try + ed = _____
4. race + s = _____
5. ride + ing = _____
6. stop + ed = _____
7. fry + ing = _____
8. sit + ing = _____
9. teach + es = _____
10. hurry + s = _____

Circle the word that completes each sentence. Write the word on the line

11. Marie is _____ because she hurt her knee.   cring   crying   cryying

12. Mark _____ an ice bag to Marie's knee.   press   presses   presss

13. Then Mark _____ a cup of tea for Marie.   makes   makees   make

14. Marie _____ her eyes and smiles.   drys   dryed   dries

15. She _____ Mark for helping her.   thanks   thankes   thankkes

Name _____

Unit 5: Inflectional Endings -**s**, -**es**, -**ed**, and -**ing**

129

Add **er** or **est** to each base word to follow the directions in each column. Write the new word on the line.

RULES Add **er** to a base word to compare two things. Add **est** to compare more than two things.
- fast, fast**er**, fast**est**
- big, big**ger**, big**gest**
- cute, cut**er**, cut**est**
- icy, ic**ier**, ic**iest**

	Base word	Compare two	Compare more than two
1.	small		
2.	thin		
3.	large		
4.	happy		
5.	safe		
6.	cold		
7.	sad		
8.	early		
9.	blue		
10.	tiny		

Add **er** or **est** to the base word at the right to complete each sentence. Write the word on the line.

11. I gave the _____ of my three apples to Toby. **big**

12. Toby ate her apple much _____ than I ate mine. **fast**

13. It was the _____ apple I have ever seen. **juicy**

14. Toby said I was the _____ person in our class. **nice**

Unit 5: Inflectional Endings -er and -est

Help your child compare family members. Make a list of who is taller and tallest, shorter and shortest, louder and loudest.

Find the word in the box that matches each clue. Write the word in the puzzle.

PHONICS and SPELLING

adult camel
clapped happiest
hopping lemon
paintbrush panda
parrot raking
rougher rowboat
telephone tried
washtub

Across

2. rough, _____, roughest
3. a tool for painting
7. something used to talk to others
8. a sour yellow fruit
10. rake + ing
12. a black and white bear
13. try + ed

Down

1. happy, happier, _____
2. a boat moved by rowing
3. a colorful bird that can talk
4. what a frog can be doing
5. a desert animal with a hump on its back
6. clap + ed
9. a tub to wash things in
11. a grown-up

Name _____

Unit 5: Spelling Compounds, Words with Schwa, and Words with Inflectional Endings

131

Find and write the word in the box that matches each clue. Then write the numbered letters in order from 1 to 9 in the spaces at the bottom of the page to answer the riddle.

carrots	flashlight	fries
highest	hurried	riding
sailboat	salad	walrus

1. a sea mammal with large tusks   _ _ _ _ _ _
                                         1

2. a small light that runs on batteries   _ _ _ _ _ _ _ _ _ _
                                                  2

3. moved quickly   _ _ _ _ _ _ _
                              3

4. lettuce, tomatoes, and dressing   _ _ _ _ _
                                          4

5. a boat that moves by wind power   _ _ _ _ _ _ _ _
                                              5

6. cooks in hot oil   _ _ _ _ _
                    6

7. traveling on horseback   _ _ _ _ _ _
                              7

8. long orange vegetables   _ _ _ _ _ _ _
                                        8

9. farthest above the ground   _ _ _ _ _ _ _
                                      9

Why does Suzy Shrimp care only about herself?

She is 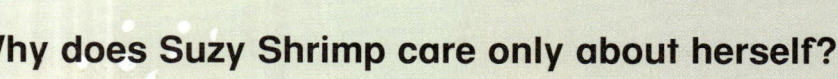.
        1 2 3 4 5 6 7 8 9

Unit 5: Compounds, Schwa, and Inflectional Endings Review

Have your child use each of the nine words above in a sentence.

Read the passage. Then read each sentence below it. Write the word that completes each sentence.

Growing Your Own Vegetables

The family grocery bill is too high. How can you help? By growing your own food!

You can grow tomatoes, lettuce, carrots, onions, and cucumbers. Vegetables will grow in tin cans, milk cartons, and even in wastebaskets. First, clean the container. Then punch holes in the bottom of it. The smaller the holes, the better. Fill the container with potting soil. Follow the directions on the seed packet to plant the seeds. You can also buy baby plants and plant them. Plant small vegetables in the smallest containers. Plant large vegetables in the largest containers.

Look for a spot with plenty of sunshine. You might try a fire escape, porch, or window box. Place the containers in the sunniest spot you find.

It is important to water the plants every day. You may also want to use plant food. Feed this to the plants every two weeks. Soon you and your family will be eating homegrown salads!

1. You can help your family by _____ your own food.

2. Punch holes in the _____ of each container.

3. _____ holes are better than larger holes.

4. Plant large vegetables in the _____ containers.

5. Put the containers in a spot with plenty of _____.

6. You will be eating _____ salads soon.

Name _____

Unit 5: Reading Compounds, Words with Schwa, and Words with Inflectional Endings in Context

133

How do you help your family or your friends? Write a how-to paragraph telling one way to be helpful. Explain what to do and list the steps needed to do it. The words in box may help you.

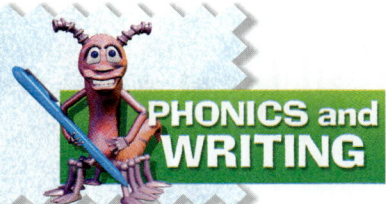

adult	alone	backyard	children	happier
homework	making	newspaper	nicest	problems
safest	shovel	teaches	telephone	upstairs

Find the word in the box that names each picture. Write the word on the line. Then say the word. Listen for the number of vowel sounds you hear. Write the number of syllables in the small box.

RULE Compound words have at least two syllables. To divide a compound word into syllables, start by dividing it between the two words that make it up.
fire|place   row|boat

baseball	beard	birdhouse	cheer
dime	jeep	notebook	paintbrush
prize	rosebud	rowboat	train

1.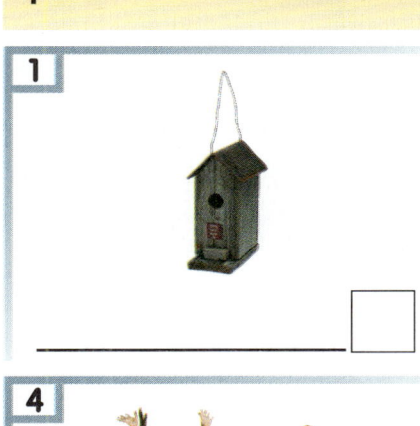
2.
3.
4.
5.
6.
7.
8.
9.
10.
11.
12.

Say each word. Listen for vowel sounds. Write the word on the line. If the word is a compound word, draw a line to divide it into syllables.

1. doghouse _____
2. care _____
3. trip _____
4. someone _____
5. sidewalk _____
6. wolf _____
7. postcard _____
8. outside _____

Find the word above that completes each sentence. Write the word on the line.

9. Sam took _____ of the Lopez's pets while the family was away.

10. Every morning Sam walked up the _____ to the Lopez's house.

11. He fed the cat and put it _____.

12. Sam always found the dog asleep in the _____.

13. Mrs. Lopez sent Sam a _____ from the Grand Canyon.

14. She said it was nice to know _____ like Sam.

15. The Lopezes trust Sam when they take a _____.

Help your child make a list of compound words. Have your child divide them into syllables.

136 Unit 5: Syllables

Write each word. Then draw a line to divide the word into syllables.

RULE If two or more consonants are between two vowels in a word, usually divide the word between the first two consonants.
fol|low   sur|prise

1. office _____
2. magnet _____
3. popping _____
4. complete _____
5. butter _____
6. basket _____
7. improve _____
8. number _____
9. mistake _____
10. corner _____

Say the words in the box. Write each word in the correct column below. Then draw a line to divide each two-syllable word into syllables.

| balloon | cape | dress | elbow | green |
| hammer | juice | nut | person | picnic |

One-Syllable Words **Two-Syllable Words**

_____   _____
_____   _____
_____   _____
_____   _____
_____   _____

Name _____

Unit 5: Syllables in VCCV and VCCCV Words

Write each word. Then draw a line to divide the word into syllables.

1. carpet _____
2. center _____
3. chimney _____
4. garden _____
5. children _____
6. ladder _____
7. window _____
8. monkey _____

Find and write a word from above that completes each sentence. Then use the letters in the shaded boxes to answer the question below.

9. Tammy brings a book to the day care _____.

10. The _____ come in from the playground to see her.

11. They sit on the _____ around Tammy.

12. They hear about a monkey who climbs a _____ to a roof.

13. The monkey walks across the roof and then goes down a _____.

14. She sees an open _____ and climbs back outside.

15. The monkey eats some lettuce from a _____.

What is Tammy doing with the children? _____

138 Unit 5: Syllables in VCCV and VCCCV Words

Help your child write an ending to the story about the monkey. Have your child point out the words with two syllables.

Write each word. Then draw a line to divide the word into syllables.

RULE If the first vowel sound in a word is **short**, usually divide the word **after** the next consonant.
shad|ow

1. timid _____
2. menu _____
3. magic _____
4. travel _____
5. boxer _____
6. lemon _____
7. honor _____
8. salad _____

Read each clue. Find the word in the box that completes the answer. Write the word on the line.

| balance | camel | dragon | palace |
| polish | river | robin | stomach |

9. I have feathers and like to sing.
I am a _____.

10. I am full of flowing water.
I am a _____.

11. I am full after you eat.
I am a _____.

12. You use me to shine your shoes.
I am shoe _____.

13. You need me if you don't want to fall off your bike.
I am good _____.

14. I breathe fire!
I am a _____.

15. I am a home for a king and queen.
I am a _____.

16. I live in the desert and have a hump.
I am a _____.

Write each word. Then draw a line to divide the word into syllables.

RULE If the first vowel sound in a word is **long,** usually divide the word **before** the next consonant.
ho|tel

1. bacon _____
2. climate _____
3. sofa _____
4. motel _____
5. label _____
6. taken _____
7. razor _____
8. robot _____

Read each clue. Find the word in the box that completes the answer. Write the word on the line.

| baby | baker | gravy | paper |
| pilot | pupil | spider | tiger |

9. I fly an airplane.
   I am a _____.

10. I am a sauce for meat or potatoes.
    I am _____.

11. I am a very young human.
    I am a _____.

12. I am a learner.
    I am a _____.

13. I am something to write on.
    I am a sheet of _____.

14. I make breads and cakes.
    I am a _____.

15. I have eight legs and spin a web.
    I am a _____.

16. I am a large cat with a striped coat.
    I am a _____.

Unit 5: Syllables in Words with Long Vowels

Think of clues for some of the words in items 1–8 and have your child guess the answers.

Read each word. Circle the vowel that is sounded alone. Then write the word and draw a line or lines to divide it into syllables.

RULE If a vowel is sounded alone in a word, usually divide the word so that the vowel forms a syllable by itself.
a|head   gas|o|line

1. alone _____
2. ocean _____
3. marathon _____
4. unit _____
5. oven _____
6. adult _____
7. asleep _____
8. popular _____
9. electric _____
10. separate _____
11. Mexico _____
12. capital _____

Write each word from above in the correct column.

Two-Syllable Words	Three-Syllable Words
_____	_____
_____	_____
_____	_____
_____	_____
_____	_____
_____	_____

Name _____

Unit 5: Syllables in Words with Vowels Sounded Alone

141

Write each word. Then draw a line or lines to divide the word into syllables.

1. apartment _____
2. open _____
3. radio _____
4. holiday _____
5. icy _____
6. telephone _____
7. odor _____
8. agreed _____
9. around _____
10. echo _____

Find the word above that completes each sentence. Write the word on the line.

11. Mr. Lee smelled something good outside his _____.

12. It was the _____ of cookies baking.

13. Then Mr. Lee heard his _____ ring.

14. He turned down his _____ and answered the phone.

15. "Hello, Mr. Lee. Today is a _____," Gloria said.

16. "It is too _____ and cold to go out," Mr. Lee said.

17. "When I come upstairs, _____ your door," Gloria said.

18. Mr. Lee heard Gloria's footsteps _____ in the hall.

19. She peeked _____ the corner and held out a tray of cookies.

20. Mr. Lee and Gloria _____ that the cookies were delicious.

Help your child think of other words with vowels that are sounded alone. Ask your child to divide the words into syllables.

Write each word. Then draw a line or lines to divide the word into syllables.

> **RULE** If two vowels are together in a word and each has its own sound, usually divide the word between the two vowels.
> gi|ant

1. idea _____
2. lion _____
3. violin _____
4. rodeo _____
5. ruin _____
6. poet _____
7. patio _____
8. create _____
9. poem _____
10. science _____
11. pioneer _____
12. usual _____

Write each word from above in the correct column.

Two-Syllable Words

_____
_____
_____
_____
_____
_____
_____

Three-Syllable Words

_____
_____
_____
_____
_____
_____
_____

Name _____

Find the word in the box that matches each clue. The number in parentheses after each clue tells how many syllables the word has. Write the word in the puzzle.

area
cereal
diary
February
giant
gymnasium
January
patio
piano
radio
violin
violet

Across

3. a large, strong person (2)
6. a breakfast food (3)
7. a machine that plays music (3)
9. a certain piece of land or space (3)
10. a place to sit outside (3)
11. a musical instrument with a keyboard (3)
12. a special room for games and sports (4)

Down

1. the first month of the year (4)
2. a purple flower (3)
4. the second month of the year (4)
5. a fiddle (3)
8. a book to write in each day (3)

Unit 5: Syllables in Words with Two Vowels Sounded Separately

Have your child use each of the words from the box in a sentence.

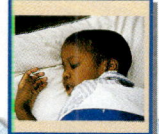    

asleep   melon   pencil   circus   elephant

RULE If a vowel is in an unstressed syllable, the vowel often has the **schwa** sound.

Write each word. Draw a line or lines to divide the word into syllables. Then circle the vowel that has the schwa sound.

1. across _____
2. valentine _____
3. children _____
4. eleven _____
5. scientist _____
6. happen _____
7. zebra _____
8. lemon _____
9. apricot _____
10. magazine _____
11. banana _____
12. wagon _____

Write each word from above in the correct column.

Two-Syllable Words

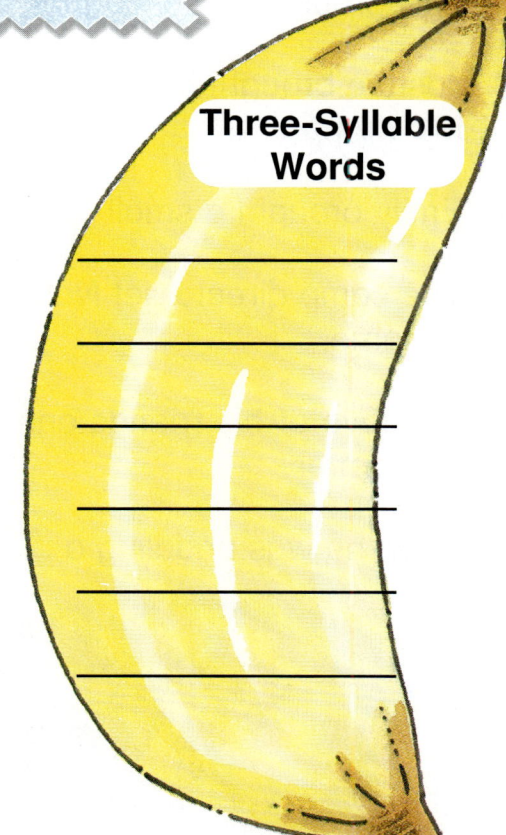

Three-Syllable Words

Name _____

Unit 5: Syllables in Words with Schwa

Find the word in the box that completes each sentence. Write the word on the line. Then circle the vowel or vowels that stand for the schwa sound. Write the number of syllables in the word on the line at the right.

| alone | cactus | camel | canoe | chicken | counselor |
| family | fossil | present | problem | seven | telephone |

1. Nathan lay all _____ in his cabin at camp. _____

2. "I have a _____," he said. "I am sick." _____

3. A camp _____ knocked on the door. _____

4. She brought Nathan a bowl of _____ soup. _____

5. Then a group of _____ campers came. _____

6. Each one brought a _____ to cheer Nathan up. _____

7. Luis brought a rock that had a _____ in it. _____

8. Joshua brought his stuffed _____ that had two humps. _____

9. Emily brought a small _____ in a pot. _____

10. The camp director let Nathan _____ his parents at home. _____

11. The love of his friends and _____ helped Nathan feel better. _____

12. Soon he was paddling a _____ around the lake. _____

Help your child find other words with the schwa sound in the sentences above.

Say each picture name. Write the word. Then draw a line to divide the word into syllables.

RULES When a word ends in a consonant and **le**, the **le** helps to make another syllable.

- If two **consonants** come before the **le**, divide the word between the two consonants. The vowel sound before the two consonants is usually short.
    bub|ble
- If a **vowel** and a consonant come before the **le**, divide the word between the vowel and the consonant. The vowel sound before the **le** is usually long.
    ma|ple

1. _____ 
2. _____ 
3. _____ 
4. _____ 
5. _____ 
6. _____ 
7. _____ 
8. _____ 
9. _____ 
10. _____ 
11. _____ 
12. _____

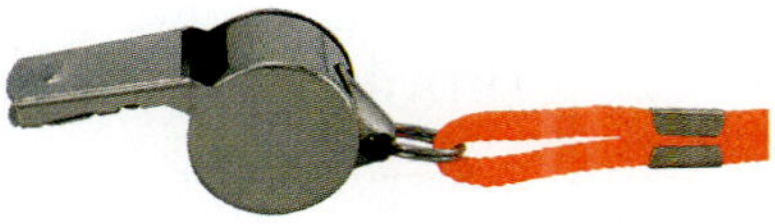

Circle the word that completes each sentence. Write the word on the line.

1. Lacy knows how to repair broken _____.
   bicycles   bristles   battles

2. She puts a reflector shaped like a _____ on each bike for safety.
   triangle   tickle   tackle

3. Lacy is really good at fixing broken _____.
   halftime   handlebars   handfuls

4. She sets up a _____ with all her tools at her school.
   title   table   topple

5. Lacy also goes to the _____ school and fixes bikes.
   muddle   muffle   middle

6. Lacy parks the bikes in a _____ on the school lawn.
   candle   cuddle   circle

7. She asks with a _____, "Any more bikes to fix?"
   giggle   gentle   gaggle

8. Eddie's little brother has broken a wheel off of his _____.
   trickle   tricycle   trample

9. "Will you be _____ to fix this?" he asks.
   amble   addle   able

10. "I can fix a _____ wheel like this in no time!" says Lacy.
    little   brittle   griddle

Unit 5: Syllables in Words That End in *-le*

Have your child select five of the incorrect word choices and use each in a sentence.

Add the ending to each base word and write the new word. Listen for vowel sounds as you say the new word. Write the number of syllables in the word.

RULE If an ending contains a vowel that is sounded, the ending forms a syllable. For example, **hopped** has only one syllable because the **e** is not sounded. **Hopping** has two syllables because the **i** is sounded.

		New Word	Number of Syllables
1.	cry + s =		
2.	drop + ing =		
3.	name + ed =		
4.	stop + ed =		
5.	fry + ing =		
6.	race + s =		
7.	run + ing =		
8.	paste + ed =		
9.	sweet + er =		
10.	short + est =		
11.	long + est =		
12.	big + er =		
13.	grade + ed =		
14.	dark + est =		
15.	dry + ed =		
16.	tell + s =		
17.	walk + ing =		
18.	brave + er =		

Name _____

Unit 5: Syllables in Words with Inflectional Endings

Circle the word that completes each sentence. Write the word on the line.

1. It must be the _____ day of the year! coldest colder cold

2. Michelle _____ a package of cocoa. opens open opening

3. She is _____ the cocoa for her little brother and sister. making makes make

4. They were busy _____ a snowman in the park. builds build building

5. She puts the cocoa in the _____ mugs she can find. big biggest bigger

6. She _____ the mugs into the family room. carrying carry carries

7. It is the _____ room in the house. warmer warming warmest

8. Michelle _____ that the cocoa will warm them up. hoping hopes hope

Look at the word choices for each sentence above. Write each two-syllable word below.

Unit 5: Syllables in Words with Inflectional Endings

Help your child identify the base word in each word choice and then add as many endings to each word as possible.

Read each word. Write the number of syllables in the word.

1. alone ____
2. capital ____
3. center ____
4. elephant ____
5. eleven ____
6. follow ____
7. hottest ____
8. juggle ____
9. toad ____
10. robin ____
11. sidewalk ____
12. tiger ____
13. trip ____
14. trying ____
15. violet ____

Each word above is in the puzzle. Find and circle each word. The words go across and down.

t	o	a	d	e	t	i	g	e	r	t
r	p	e	l	e	v	e	n	n	e	r
v	h	y	t	r	y	i	n	g	f	i
i	o	c	a	p	i	t	a	l	e	p
o	t	r	s	i	d	e	w	a	l	k
l	t	o	v	j	c	e	n	t	e	r
e	e	b	i	u	p	g	o	f	p	r
t	s	i	e	g	r	t	i	i	h	v
e	t	n	l	g	c	m	e	p	a	l
v	f	o	l	l	o	w	r	p	n	o
a	l	o	n	e	s	i	d	q	t	w

Unit 5: Syllables Review

Find the word in the box that matches each clue. Then write the numbered letters in order from 1 to 11 in the spaces below to answer the riddle.

| asleep | baker | carpet | doghouse | giggling | piano |
| pilot | pioneer | river | sofa | turtle | |

1. I make breads and cakes. __ __ __ __ __
                                                1

2. You can play me. __ __ __ __ __
                                 2

3. You are this when you nap. __ __ __ __ __ __
                                1

4. I am like a rug. __ __ __ __ __ __
                              4

5. I am bigger than a stream. __ __ __ __ __
                                   5

6. I went west in a wagon. __ __ __ __ __ __ __
                                        6

7. I follow tickling. __ __ __ __ __ __ __ __
                            7

8. I am also called a couch. __ __ __ __
                                  8

9. I fly an airplane. __ __ __ __ __
                        9

10. I have a shell on my back. __ __ __ __ __ __
                                     10

11. A dog might live in me. __ __ __ __ __ __ __ __
                                         11

When is a campfire like a lion?

When it is a __ __ __ __ __ __ __   __ __ __ __ !
             1 2 3 4 5 6 7   8 9 10 11

152 Unit 5: Syllables Review

AT HOME — Have your child show you how to divide the words from the box into syllables.

Say each picture name. Write the word on the line.

RULES A **plural** is a word that means more than one. Add **s** to most words to make them plural. If the word ends in **ch, s, sh, ss, x,** or **z,** add **es**.
book**s**   brush**es**   fox**es**

1.  _____
2.  _____
3.  _____
4.  _____
5.  _____
6.  _____
7.  _____
8.  _____

Circle the plural in each sentence. Then write the singular form of the word on the line.

9. Ping took two buses to get to the hospital. _____

10. He brought some gifts to his sick cousin. _____

11. Ping gave her flowers, too. _____

12. His cousin ate the grapes that Ping brought. _____

13. Ping also brought books for his cousin to read. _____

14. He brought her paper and brushes so she could paint. _____

15. Ping's cousin thanked him for the presents. _____

Name _____

Read the word under each picture. Write its plural on the line.

RULES Change the spelling of some words to form the plural.
- If a word ends with a consonant and **y**, change the **y** to **i** and add **es**.
  pen**y**   penn**ies**
- If a word ends in **f** or **fe**, change **f** or **fe** to **v** and add **es**.
  wol**f**   wol**ves**

1.  puppy _____
2.  leaf _____
3. 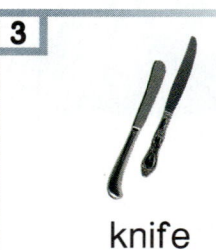 knife _____
4.  cherry _____

Read each pair of sentences. Complete the second sentence by making the underlined word in the first sentence plural.

5. Mom went to the <u>grocery</u> store.

   I put away the bags of _____ for her.

6. I took the book off the <u>shelf</u>.

   The library has many _____ of books.

7. A baby cow is called a <u>calf</u>.

   There are five _____ in the field.

8. This is the best day of my <u>life</u>!

   They say that a cat has nine _____.

9. I see a <u>daisy</u> growing in the yard.

   I will pick a bunch of _____ for Mom.

10. Mom baked a <u>blueberry</u> pie.

    We picked the _____ for her.

Name an object in your home. Have your child write and read the plural form of the word.

Unit 5: Plurals

Read the two words. Then write the contraction for them on the line.

RULE A contraction is two words put together to make one word. Use an **apostrophe** (') to show where letters are left out.
   is not = isn't
• Two exceptions:
   cannot = can't
   will not = won't

is + not = isn't

1. you + will = _____
2. we + will = _____
3. you + have = _____
4. I + have = _____
5. will + not = _____
6. could + not = _____
7. he + is = _____
8. she + is = _____
9. you + are = _____
10. they + are = _____
11. I + am = _____
12. cannot = _____

Read each contraction. Write the two words that make up the contraction.

13. didn't = _____ + _____
14. we've = _____ + _____
15. wouldn't = _____ + _____
16. they'll = _____ + _____
17. there's = _____ + _____
18. we're = _____ + _____
19. aren't = _____ + _____
20. won't = _____ + _____

will + not = won't

Name _____

Read the story. Circle each contraction and write it below. Then write the two words that make up the contraction.

Taking Care of Dusty

Heather's dog Dusty didn't feel well. Dusty hadn't been eating. Heather and her mom took Dusty to the vet. The vet gave Dusty some medicine to take.

"I'm going to give Dusty his medicine," Heather said. "I'll take care of him. I've done it before."

"I know you will," Mom said.

Heather brought Dusty water. Dusty wouldn't drink it. Heather brought Dusty a blanket. Dusty lay on the blanket.

"You'll like this," Heather said. She gave Dusty his medicine.

Heather did a good job of taking care of Dusty. In the morning he ate his food. Soon he wanted to go out and play.

"He's all better!" Heather said.

"It's because you took good care of him," said Mom. "You're a good pet owner."

	Contraction	Two Words	
1.	_____	_____ + _____	
2.	_____	_____ + _____	
3.	_____	_____ + _____	
4.	_____	_____ + _____	
5.	_____	_____ + _____	
6.	_____	_____ + _____	
7.	_____	_____ + _____	
8.	_____	_____ + _____	
9.	_____	_____ + _____	
10.	_____	_____ + _____	

Unit 5: Contractions

Have your child read the story aloud substituting two words in place of each contraction.

Change each group of words to its possessive form. Write the possessive on the line.

> **RULE** A **possessive** is a word that shows ownership. Add an **apostrophe** (') and an **s** to show that something or someone has or owns something.
> the dog**'s** bone

1. the cookies that Emily has _____
2. the skateboard that the boy owns _____
3. the shirt that Taylor owns _____
4. the mitt that Vanessa has _____
5. the purse that Yuko owns _____
6. the leash that the dog has _____

Circle the word that completes each sentence. Write the word on the line.

7. _____ friend Marc was having trouble with math.   Tony   Tony's

8. Tony rode his _____ bike over to do homework with Marc.   sister's   sisters

9. Marc found pencils on his _____ desk.   dads   dad's

10. _____ juice spilled on their papers.   Marcs   Marc's

11. Only one _____ homework stayed dry.   boy's   boys

12. Marc got more paper from his _____ notebook.   aunt's   aunts

13. Marc shook his _____ hand to thank him.   friends   friend's

Name _____

Unit 5: Singular Possessives

Change each group of words to its possessive form. Write the possessive on the line.

RULE To show that more than one person or thing owns or has something, you usually add an **apostrophe** (') **after** the final **s**. The boy**s**' bikes are the bikes that two or more boys have.

1. the legs of the giraffes _____
2. the beds where the twins sleep _____
3. the desks where the students sit _____
4. the uniforms that the teams wear _____
5. the covers of the books _____
6. the skins of the bananas _____

Circle the word that completes each sentence. Write the word on the line.

7. Matt went into both of his _____ bedrooms.
   brothers   brother's   brothers'

8. He picked up many pairs of the _____ shoes.
   boy's   boys'   boys

9. Then he put fresh water in the _____ cages.
   gerbil's   gerbils'   gerbils

10. Matt put away the two _____ chew toys.
    puppies   puppie's   puppies'

11. Then he hung his _____ shirts in their closets.
    sisters'   sister's   sisters

Unit 5: Plural Possessives

Ask your child to draw pictures to illustrate some of the phrases at the top of the page.

Use the clues and the words in the box to complete the puzzle. Then read down the squares and write the answer to the question.

babies	bee's	bottles	boys'	calves
can't	circles	days	he's	matches
she'll	shouldn't	turkeys	won't	you've

1. used to make fire
2. day + s
3. owned by boys
4. calf + s
5. he + is
6. will + not
7. you + have
8. should + not
9. containers
10. baby + s
11. cannot
12. round shapes
13. she + will
14. owned by a bee
15. Thanksgiving birds

Who is one of the most helpful people you know?

Name _____

Unit 5: Spelling Plurals, Contractions, and Possessives

Read each clue. Unscramble the word under it to find the answer. Write the word on the line.

1. the boots that belong to Sara

   r'saaS _____ boots

2. the contraction for *did not*

   idnd't _____

3. tree parts that fall off in autumn

   sveela _____

4. more than one brush

   srebush _____

5. the contraction for *they are*

   rethy'e _____

6. shapes with three sides

   ritlesang _____

7. owned by the teams

   m'atse _____

8. the plural of *half*

   valesh _____

9. machines that play music

   odrisa _____

10. newborns

    eabibs _____

11. the plural of *guess*

    ussegse _____

12. openings in a house

    dowsniw _____

13. baby dogs

    pipsepu _____

14. the contraction for *you have*

    uv'yeo _____

160 Unit 5: Plurals, Contractions, and Possessives Review

AT HOME Write each family member's name. Have your child divide each name into syllables and then write each in its possessive form.

Read the passage. Then read the sentences below it. Write the word that completes each sentence.

Who's a Good Helper?

Many people work as helpers. Firefighters help by putting out fires. They use ladders to get people and pets out of burning buildings.

Coaches help their teams learn how to play sports. The players' skills get better with the coach's help. A swimming coach can teach children and adults to swim better and faster.

Ambulance drivers are helpers. They help people who are sick or hurt. They don't waste time when someone needs their help.

A vet doesn't help people who are sick. Vets help puppies, kittens, and other pets. They take care of animals who are sick or hurt.

Bus drivers help children get to and from school. Taxi drivers help people go to work, to the store, and to places to have fun. Pilots don't drive buses or cars. They fly planes. Their job is to help people travel long distances.

Maybe you're a helper, too. Do you ever help your friends at school? Do you help your teacher? How can you be a helper today?

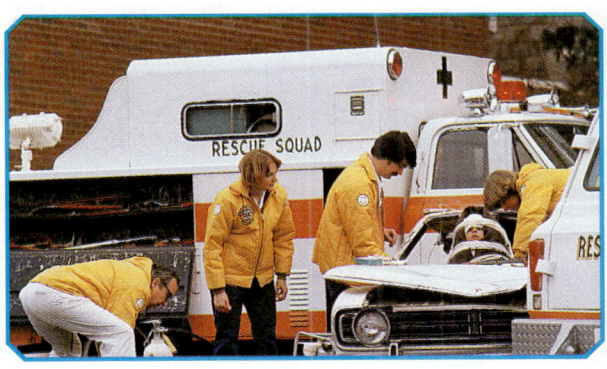

1. Firefighters help people and pets get out of burning _____.

2. _____ teach teams how to play sports.

3. Players can do better at sports with a _____ help.

4. A vet _____ help sick people.

5. Vets take care of _____, kittens, and other pets.

6. Pilots help people travel long _____.

Name _____

Unit 5: Reading Plurals, Contractions, and Possessives in Context

Can you think of other workers who are helpers? Write a paragraph about someone whose job is to help people. Tell what the person does and how the person's job helps others. The words in the box may help you.

able	around	brother's	exercise	family
garden	hammer	middle	paintbrush	paper
science	sidewalk	someone	train	we're

Find the word in the box that names each picture. Write the word on the line. Then circle the number of syllables in the word.

Unit 5 CHECK-UP

banana	calves	clapped	cries	dishes
laughing	notebook	pencil	piano	reaches
rowboat	salad	tiger	turtle	violin

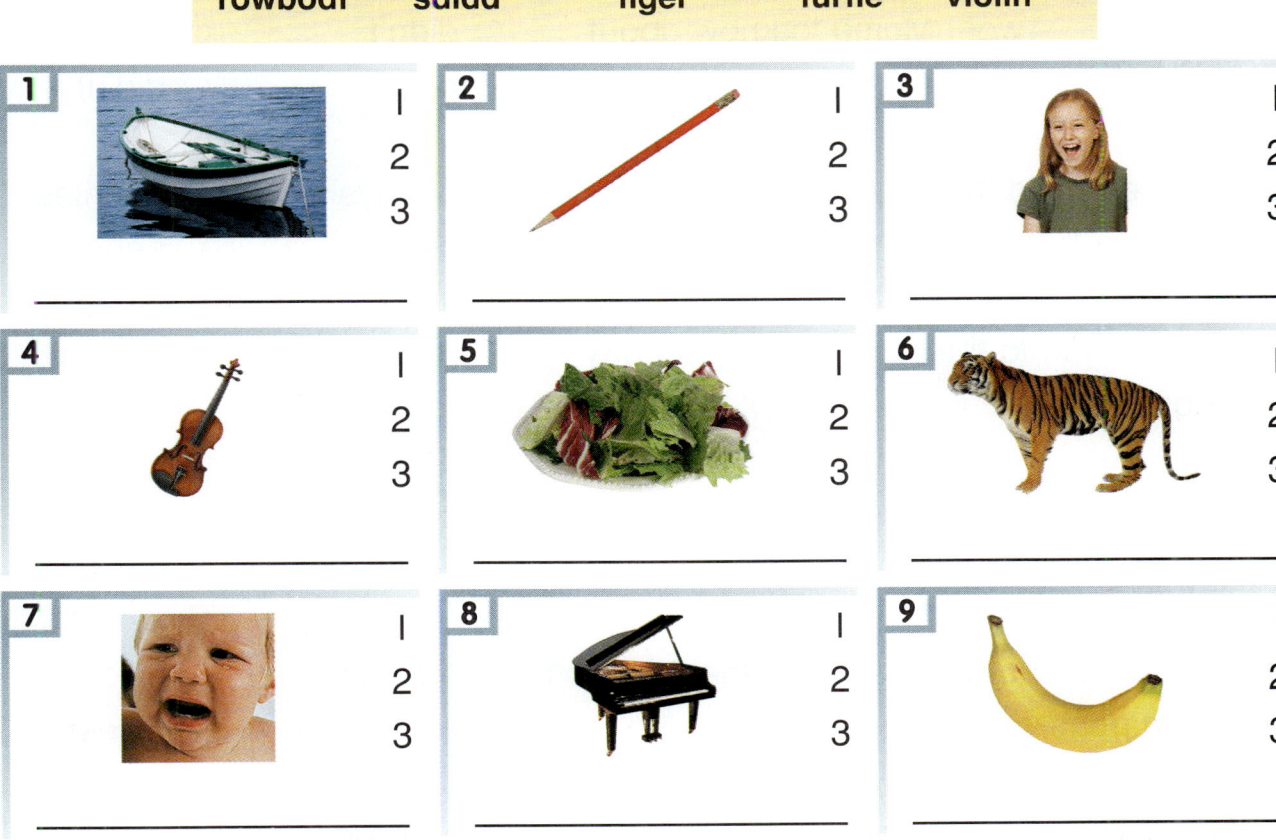

Name _____

Unit 5: Assessing Compounds, Schwa, Inflectional Endings, Syllables, and Plurals

Unit 5 CHECK-UP

Fill in the circle next to the word that completes each sentence.

1. Lupe remembered that today is _____ birthday.
   - ○ Mamas
   - ○ Mamas'
   - ○ Mama's
   - ○ Mamaes

2. Lupe _____ want Mama to know about the surprise.
   - ○ didn't
   - ○ didnt
   - ○ didn'ot
   - ○ did'nt

3. Lupe emptied the _____ and nickels from her bank.
   - ○ pennys
   - ○ penny's
   - ○ pennies
   - ○ pennes

4. She walked to the _____ market to buy eggs and milk.
   - ○ farmers
   - ○ farmed
   - ○ farmer
   - ○ farmers'

5. Lupe _____ the groceries into the house quietly.
   - ○ carryed
   - ○ cared
   - ○ carried
   - ○ carry

6. She picked out the _____ of the three frying pans.
   - ○ biggest
   - ○ bigger
   - ○ big
   - ○ bigest

7. Her dad _____ the eggs and Lupe sliced an apricot.
   - ○ cooking
   - ○ cookes
   - ○ cook
   - ○ cooked

8. Lupe spread blueberry jam on two _____ of toast.
   - ○ slicees
   - ○ slicer
   - ○ slices
   - ○ sliced

9. Mama awoke to a _____ breakfast in bed.
   - ○ baseball
   - ○ birthday
   - ○ backward
   - ○ bathtub

10. She said it was the _____ morning ever!
    - ○ happyest
    - ○ happier
    - ○ happy
    - ○ happiest

Unit 5: Assessing Compounds, Inflectional Endings, Plurals, Contractions, and Possessives

UNIT 6
Collector's Corner
Suffixes and Prefixes

from The Pancake Collector

Come visit my pancake collection,
it's unique in the civilized world.
I have pancakes of every description,
pancakes flaky and fluffy and curled.

I have pancakes of various sizes,
pancakes regular, heavy and light,
underdone pancakes and overdone pancakes,
and pancakes done perfectly right.

Jack Prelutsky

Think About It

What other kinds of pancakes could be collected?
What things do you like to collect?

Dear Family of _____,

Your child will be learning about prefixes and suffixes. Your child will be using these skills to read about collecting things. Here are some activities you can do together.

- Fold a large piece of paper into eight sections. At the top of each section, write one of the following suffixes: *-less*, *-ness*, *-ment*, *-tion*, *-able*, *-en*, *-ous*, or *-ist*. Then have your child write in each section as many words as he or she can with that suffix. Repeat the activity with the prefixes *un-*, *re-*, *dis-*, *mis-*, *pre-*, *de-*, *im-*, and *in-*.
- Play a game of Suffix-Prefix Bingo with your child. Using one of the base words shown on the grid at the right, add a prefix or suffix and say the word, such as *prepay*. Have your child put a marker on the prefix or suffix square in the correct base word column. Follow the regular rules for bingo.
- Talk with your child about what he or she likes to collect, such as baseball cards, stamps, seashells, rocks, or stickers. Have your child write a story about the hobby, using as many words with prefixes and suffixes as possible. Have your child identify the words with prefixes and suffixes.

LIBRARY LINK

You may want to visit the library and find the book *The Woman Who Saved Things* by Phyllis Krasilovsky. Read it with your child.

pay	treat	agree	connect	use
re	mis	ment	tion	ful
able	ment	able	dis	less
pre	able	dis	re	mis
ment	pre	pre	mis	able

Estimada familia de _____,

Su niño o niña aprenderá prefijos y sufijos en inglés. Él o ella usará estos conocimientos en su lectura sobre cómo hacer colecciones de cosas. Algunas actividades que usted y su niño o niña pueden hacer en inglés aparecen a continuación.

- Doble una hoja grande de papel en ocho secciones. En la parte superior de cada sección escriba los siguientes sufijos: *-less*, *-ness*, *-ment*, *-ion*, *-able*, *-en*, *-ous*, *-ist*. Luego, invite a su niño o niña a que escriba en cada sección todas las palabras con ese sufijo que pueda. Repita la actividad con los prefijos *un-*, *re-*, *dis-*, *mis-*, *pre-*, *de-*, *im-* e *in-*.
- Juntos jueguen al Bingo de sufijos y prefijos. Usen una de las palabras base que aparecen en la gráfica de arriba, agréguenle un prefijo o sufijo y luego digan la palabra, tal como en *prepay*. Pídale a su niño o niña que haga una marca en el cuadro del prefijo o sufijo de la columna correcta de la palabra base. Sigan las reglas que se aplican al juego del bingo.
- Converse con su niño o niña sobre lo que a él o ella le gusta coleccionar, como las tarjetas de béisbol, estampillas, caracoles de mar, piedras o calcomanías. Invite a su niño o niña a que escriba un cuento sobre su pasatiempo favorito y que use tantas palabras con prefijos y sufijos como sea posible. Luego pídale que identifique las palabras que tengan prefijos y sufijos.

Read each definition. Add the suffix **less, ness, y, ful,** or **ly** to the base word to make a word that matches the definition. Write the word on the line.

RULE A **suffix** is a word part added to the end of a base word to change its meaning.
- **less** means "without"
  spot**less** = without spots
- **ness** and **y** mean "having" or "the state of being"
  kind**ness** = the state of being kind
  cloud**y** = having clouds
- **ful** means "with" or "full of"
  fear**ful** = full of fear
- **ly** often means "in that way"
  sad**ly** = in a sad way

1. having rain   rain + _____ = _____
2. full of hope   hope + _____ = _____
3. the state of being fresh   fresh + _____ = _____
4. without sleep   sleep + _____ = _____
5. in a safe way   safe + _____ = _____

Find the word in the box that completes each sentence. Write the word on the line.

| brightly | careless | closely | dirty | hardness | wonderful |

6. Today the sun is shining _____.
7. It is a _____ day for collecting rocks.
8. John looks _____ at a rock he finds.
9. He taps it with a hammer to test its _____.
10. It will break if he is _____.
11. John washes the _____ rocks.

Name _____

Unit 6: Suffixes *-less, -ness, -y, -ful,* and *-ly*

Write each word on the line. Draw a line to divide the word into syllables.

RULE In a word with a suffix, the suffix makes up at least one syllable of the word.
sweet|ly   thought|less

1. helpless _____
2. windy _____
3. quickly _____
4. bravely _____
5. thoughtful _____
6. sickness _____
7. lucky _____
8. thankful _____
9. boneless _____
10. darkness _____

Circle the word that completes each sentence. Write the word on the line. Then draw a line to divide the word into syllables.

11. Mandy is _____ not to step on the rocks.   careful / careless

12. Mandy lines up the rocks _____ on a table.   neatness / neatly

13. A magnifying glass is a _____ tool for studying rocks.   useless / useful

14. People use brushes to clean _____ rocks.   dusty / dustness

15. Mandy was _____ to find a pink rock.   joyful / joyless

Unit 6: Syllables in Words with Suffixes -less, -ness, -y, -ful, and -ly

Read some words from the page aloud. Have your child write each word and draw a line between the syllables.

Add the suffix to each base word. Write the new word on the line.

RULE The suffixes **ment** and **ion** mean "the act of" or "the result of an action."
 amaze**ment** = the result of being amazed
 subtract**ion** = the act of subtracting
Drop the **e** at the end of a word before adding a suffix that begins with a vowel.
 concentrate + **ion** = concentrat**ion**

1. move + ment _____
2. create + ion _____
3. act + ion _____
4. agree + ment _____
5. suggest + ion _____
6. amuse + ment _____
7. collect + ion _____
8. elect + ion _____
9. ship + ment _____
10. improve + ment _____

Use a word above to answer each question. Write the word on the line.

11. What word names a group of things that you have gathered? _____
12. What word describes a fun park with rides? _____
13. What word names a piece of advice? _____
14. What word names an event when people vote? _____
15. What word rhymes with *fraction*? _____
16. What word names something that makes things better? _____

Name _____

Unit 6: Suffixes *-ment* and *-ion*   **169**

Find and write the word from the box that matches each definition. Then use the boxed letters to complete the sentence at the bottom of the page.

addition	completion	enjoyment
measurement	payment	placement
pollution	punishment	separation

1. the result of paying _____
2. the result of being punished _____
3. the act of adding _____
4. the result of polluting _____
5. the result of placing _____
6. the act of separating _____
7. the act of measuring _____
8. the result of completing _____
9. the act of enjoying _____

A fancy name for stamp collecting is _____.

Unit 6: Suffixes *-ment* and *-ion*

Ask your child to think of other words that end in *-ment* or *-ion*.

Each word in the box is in the puzzle. Find and circle each word. Words go across, down, forward, and backward.

RULE Remember that a suffix changes the meaning of the base word.
- **able** means "able to be"
  eras**able** = able to be erased
- **en** means "to become" or "made of"
  sharp**en** = to become sharp
- **ous** means "full of"
  danger**ous** = full of danger

bendable	famous	darken
joyous	lighten	nervous
readable	shorten	washable

```
m  i  b  e  n  d  a  b  l  e
y  s  w  l  o  a  v  n  e  k
p  i  y  b  w  r  s  e  l  c
m  b  s  a  t  k  a  r  b  t
l  i  g  h  t  e  n  v  a  j
r  e  d  s  u  n  c  o  d  o
t  h  o  a  c  s  u  u  a  y
s  x  v  w  t  n  k  s  e  o
s  h  o  r  t  e  n  c  r  u
c  o  u  r  f  a  m  o  u  s
```

Find the word in the box that completes each sentence. Write the word on the line.

adorable
golden
nervous
poisonous
wooden

1. The local zoo has a collection of _____ snakes.

2. Just looking at them makes my mom _____.

3. One is a _____ color that looks like the sun.

4. The brown one is so still that it looks _____.

5. Mom does not think that snakes are _____ animals.

Name _____

Unit 6: Suffixes -able, -en, and -ous

Add the suffix to each base word. Write the new word on the line.

RULE Remember that a **suffix** changes the meaning of a word.
er, or, and **ist** mean "a person who"
paint**er** = a person who paints
sail**or** = a person who sails
violin**ist** = a person who plays the violin

Add er

1. farm _____
2. report _____
3. photograph _____
4. play _____

Add or

5. edit _____
6. act _____
7. collect _____
8. direct _____

Add ist

9. tour _____
10. cartoon _____
11. organ _____
12. art _____

Find a word above that answers each riddle. Write the word on the line.

13. I like to buy and save trading cards. I am a _____.
14. I draw pictures for comic books. I am a _____.
15. I take pictures. I am a _____.
16. I grow the food that people eat. I am a _____.
17. I perform in movies and plays. I am an _____.
18. I like to travel for fun. I am a _____.

Unit 6: Suffixes *-er, -or,* and *-ist*

Ask your child to choose five words with suffixes from the page and use each in a sentence.

Read each definition. Add the prefix un, dis, or re to the base word to make a word that matches the definition. Write the word on the line.

> **RULE** A **prefix** is a word part added to the beginning of a base word to change its meaning.
> - **un** and **dis** mean "not" or "the opposite of"
>   **un**happy = not happy
>   **dis**order = the opposite of *order*
> - **re** means "again"
>   **re**tell = to tell again

1. the opposite of *pack* _____
2. not safe _____
3. the opposite of *comfort* _____
4. to use again _____
5. to wrap again _____
6. not known _____
7. to teach again _____
8. to dial again _____
9. the opposite of *obey* _____
10. the opposite of *appear* _____

Find the word in the box that can replace each underlined phrase. Write the word on the line.

11. Pam and I <u>do not agree</u> on which comic book is better. _____
12. I <u>do not like</u> the old ones, but she likes them the best. _____
13. Comic books are even fun to <u>read again</u>. _____
14. Sometimes I am <u>not able</u> to find the comic book that I want. _____
15. I check and then <u>check again</u> at the comic book store. _____
16. A torn comic book is <u>not equal</u> in value to one in perfect shape. _____

| recheck |
| unable |
| dislike |
| unequal |
| reread |
| disagree |

Name _____

Unit 6: Prefixes *un-*, *dis-*, and *re-*

Draw a line or lines to divide each word into syllables. Write the base word on the line.

RULE In a word with a prefix, the prefix makes up at least one syllable of the word.
dis|like   re|use

1. rewrite _____
2. untold _____
3. unmade _____
4. repay _____
5. rebuild _____
6. dishonest _____
7. distrust _____
8. unbend _____

Find the word in the box that can replace the words in parentheses. Use the word to rewrite the sentence.

| disappeared | dislike | revisit | unhappy | unlocks | unsure |

9. The new coin I bought for my collection has (opposite of *appeared*).
   _____
10. If I don't find the coin, I will be (not happy).
    _____
11. I (opposite of *like*) losing things.
    _____
12. I will (visit again) the store where I bought the coin.
    _____
13. I am (not sure) whether I left with the coin.
    _____
14. The clerk (opposite of *locks*) a cabinet and hands me my coin.
    _____

Write each word from the box in the correct column. Draw a line or lines to divide each word into syllables.

RULES Remember that a prefix changes the meaning of a word.
- **mis** means "in the wrong way" or "in a bad way"
  misspell = to spell in the wrong way
- **pre** means "before"
  prepay = to pay before
- **de** means "to remove"
  defrost = to remove frost

declaw	misuse	preview
misbehave	debone	pretest
mistreat	prewash	desalt

Words with pre
_____
_____
_____

Words with mis
_____
_____
_____

Words with de
_____
_____
_____

Use the clues below and the words in the box to complete the crossword puzzle.

Across
1. to wash before
5. to remove salt
6. to behave in a bad way
7. to remove a bone
8. to treat in a bad way

Down
1. to view before
2. to remove a claw
3. to use in the wrong way
4. to test before

Name _____

Unit 6: Prefixes *mis-*, *pre-*, and *de-*

Read each word. Write a definition on the line. Remember that im and in mean "not."

RULE Remember that a prefix changes the meaning of a word.
im and **in** mean "not"
   impossible = not possible
   inactive = not active

1. impossible _____
2. invisible _____
3. incorrect _____
4. immature _____
5. improper _____
6. impolite _____
7. impatient _____
8. independent _____
9. informal _____
10. imperfect _____
11. incomplete _____
12. inexpensive _____

Write a word from above to replace the words in parentheses under each line.

It is _____ to get into Ling's bedroom.
       (not possible)

She has so many stuffed animals! She buys small,

_____ ones at a nearby store. Some of her
(not expensive)

animals are _____, but she still loves them.
              (not perfect)

Ling thinks her collection is _____ because
                               (not complete)

she doesn't have a pink monkey. She is so _____!
                                            (not patient)

I tell her to keep looking. It is only a matter of time before she

finds one!

Unit 6: Prefixes *im-* and *in-*

Choose three words with the prefix *im-* or *in-*. Ask your child to define the base word and then the word with the prefix.

Find the word in the box that completes each sentence. Write the word on the line.

amazement	cartoonist	collection	collector
colorful	decode	disagree	hopeless
imperfect	neatly	rewrite	teacher

1. To be a _____, you need two or more of almost anything.

2. Maria has a collection of many _____ rocks.

3. To her _____, she has found many rocks in her backyard.

4. Maria displays her rocks _____ in empty egg cartons.

5. Collectors _____ on the value of autographed sports cards.

6. Some say that if a card is signed, it is an _____ example.

7. The cartoons in a comic book are drawn by a _____.

8. Gina feels _____ that she'll ever find her favorite comic book.

9. Some comic books have secret messages to _____.

10. I have been given a writing assignment by my _____.

11. I have to write a paragraph about my stamp _____.

12. If there are spelling errors, I'll have to _____ it.

Unit 6: Spelling Words with Suffixes and Prefixes

Read each definition. Use a suffix from the box to complete the word that matches the definition.

1. the result of agreeing   agree_____
2. without hope   h(o)pe_____
3. full of care   (c)are_____
4. to become light   (l)igh(t)___
5. able to be washed   wash_____
6. in a nice way   (n)i(c)e___

Suffixes
able
ful
ly
en
less
ment

Read each definition. Use a prefix from the box to complete the word that matches the definition.

7. not formal   ___forma(l)
8. to wrap again   ___wrap
9. not proper   ___pr(o)per
10. not safe   ___saf(e)
11. to mix before   ___m(i)x
12. to use in a wrong way   ___use

Prefixes
im
mis
re
in
pre
un

Now write all the circled letters in the space below. Unscramble the letters to make a word. Write the letters on the lines.

Answer: _____

Ask your child to think of other base words and add some of these suffixes and prefixes to them.

178   Unit 6: Suffixes and Prefixes Review

Read the passage. Then read the sentences below it. Write the word that completes each sentence.

PHONICS and READING

So Many Collections!

Collecting is an enjoyable activity for many people. Each collection has its own special story. People who love the outdoors may collect things from nature, such as rocks, shells, or leaves. Travelers may collect bumper stickers, T-shirts, or mugs. Some collectors get autographs of famous people. These collectors write to sports stars, movie actors, scientists, artists, and people in government.

Stamp collecting is one of the world's most popular hobbies. There are many different kinds of stamps all over the world. Some collectors collect stamps with animal pictures on them. Others save stamps with colorful flowers or birds from around the world.

Our world is changing fast. Some collectors help keep history alive. By keeping collections of items from one period of time, they help us remember what the past was like.

1. Many people find collecting _____.

2. _____ sometimes collect T-shirts.

3. Autograph collectors write to many _____ people.

4. Some write to sports stars or to people in _____.

5. Some stamp collectors focus on _____ flowers.

6. Some _____ help keep history alive.

Name _____

Unit 6: Reading Words with Suffixes and Prefixes in Context

If you made a stamp, what would it look like? Would it show a person, a place, or a thing? Draw a picture of your stamp. Then write a paragraph telling about it. The words in the box may help you.

addition
adorable
brightly
cartoonist
colorful
enjoyment
location
relive
surely
wonderful

___

Unit 6: Writing Words with Suffixes and Prefixes

Ask your child to read the paragraph aloud.

Circle the word that completes each sentence. Write the word on the line.

1. Something that is not correct is _____.
   - correctly
   - correctable
   - incorrect

2. To remove a king from his throne is to _____ him.
   - rethrone
   - dethrone
   - throneless

3. My book collection has given me hours of _____.
   - unenjoy
   - enjoyable
   - enjoyment

4. To heat the oven before you cook is to _____ it.
   - reheat
   - preheat
   - heater

5. The sky is gray and it has been raining _____ all day.
   - lightly
   - lighten
   - lightness

6. My mother displays her doll _____ in the living room.
   - collection
   - collector
   - collectable

7. To paint again is to _____.
   - painter
   - paintless
   - repaint

8. An _____ performs in movies or in plays.
   - action
   - actor
   - react

9. Jill is always _____ to wear her helmet when she rides her bike.
   - careful
   - miscare
   - careless

10. To put in a wrong place is to _____.
    - placement
    - misplace
    - replace

Name _____

Unit 6: Assessing Suffixes and Prefixes

Unit 6 CHECK-UP — Fill in the circle next to the word that completes the sentence.

1. Digging up rocks is a _____ job.
   - ○ messy
   - ○ snowy
   - ○ windy
   - ○ rainy

2. I tripped on a rock on the _____ path.
   - ○ undo
   - ○ unhappy
   - ○ uneven
   - ○ unlike

3. Our science _____ told us that there are three kinds of rocks.
   - ○ teachable
   - ○ teacher
   - ○ reteach
   - ○ teaching

4. I used a shovel to _____ rocks on the beach.
   - ○ unsafe
   - ○ unhurt
   - ○ uncover
   - ○ unafraid

5. Be careful not to _____ words on your spelling test.
   - ○ misspell
   - ○ mistrust
   - ○ misbehave
   - ○ mislead

6. You must be a creative person to be an _____.
   - ○ invention
   - ○ reinvent
   - ○ invented
   - ○ inventor

7. A sports star at the mall caused a lot of _____.
   - ○ shipment
   - ○ excitement
   - ○ development
   - ○ movement

8. The sports star treated everyone with _____.
   - ○ unkind
   - ○ kindness
   - ○ kindly
   - ○ kinds

9. I was _____ that she gave me her autograph.
   - ○ hurtful
   - ○ handful
   - ○ thankful
   - ○ helpful

10. It wasn't _____ to get it after all.
    - ○ impossible
    - ○ imperfect
    - ○ invisible
    - ○ incomplete

UNIT 7
At Home

Dictionary Skills, Multiple-Meaning Words, Synonyms, Antonyms, Homonyms

Pick Up Your Room

Pick up your room, my mother says
   (She says it every day);
My room's too heavy to pick up
   (That's what I always say).

Drink up your milk, she says to me,
   Don't bubble like a clown;
Of course she knows I'll answer that
   I'd rather drink it down.

And when she says at eight o'clock,
   You must go right to bed,
We both repeat my answer:
   Why not go left instead?

Mary Ann Hoberman

Think About It

How is the speaker having fun with his or her mother? What other sayings have two meanings?

Dear Family of _____,

Your child will be learning dictionary skills; multiple-meaning words, such as *batter* and *watch*; synonyms, such as *happy* and *glad*; antonyms such as *smile* and *frown*; and homonyms, such as *meat* and *meet*. Your child will be using these skills to read about the theme At Home. Here are some activities you can do together.

- Before a family meal, discuss each item being served. Have your child write a menu listing the items in alphabetical order, such as *apple juice, bread, chicken, rice,* and *salad*. Then have your child serve the meal in alphabetical order.
- Have your child create a personal dictionary of words with multiple meanings, such as *match* and *cold*. Your child may wish to illustrate each definition.
- Challenge your child to use a dictionary to find as many synonyms as he or she can for words such as *fast, run,* and *cold*.

LIBRARY LINK

You might like to visit the library and find the book *Our Home Is the Sea* by Dennis Luzak. Read it with your child.

Estimada familia de _____,

Su niño o niña aprenderá destrezas para el uso del diccionario; palabras de varios significados, tales como *batter* y *watch*; sinónimos, tales como *happy* y *glad*; antónimos, tales como *smile* y *frown*; además de homónimos, tales como *meat* y *meet*. Su niño o niña usará estos conocimientos en su lectura sobre el tema En casa (At Home). Algunas actividades que usted y su niño o niña pueden hacer en inglés aparecen a continuación.

- Antes de la cena familiar, conversen sobre cada comestible que se sirve. Invite a su niño o niña a que escriba el menú haciendo una lista de los artículos en orden alfabético, como *apple juice, bread, chicken, rice* y *ensalada*. Luego invite a su niño o niña a que sirva la cena en orden alfabético.
- Invite a su niño o niña a que organice un diccionario personal de palabras con varios significados, tales como *match* y *cold*. Tal vez él o ella quisiera acompañar cada definición con un dibujo.
- Rete a su niño o niña a que use el diccionario para encontrar tantos sinónimos como pueda para palabras como *fast, run* y *cold*.

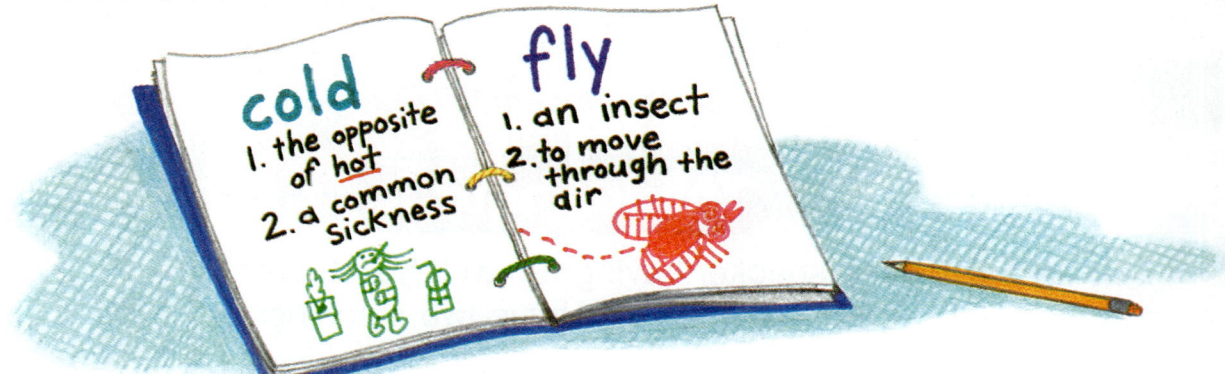

Unit 7: Family Involvement

Lee and Len want to put their shopping list in alphabetical order. Write the words in each group in alphabetical order.

RULE Words in the dictionary are listed in **alphabetical order**.
- When words begin with the **same** letter, use the **second** letter to put them in alphabetical order.
  pears   prunes
- When words begin with the **same two** letters, use the **third** letter to put them in alphabetical order.
  salad   sandwich

1
asparagus _____
apples   _____
almonds   _____

2
beef   _____
beans   _____
berries   _____

3
biscuits   _____
butter   _____
bread   _____

4
chocolate _____
chili   _____
cheese   _____

5
codfish   _____
cornflakes _____
coffee   _____

6
flour   _____
fruit   _____
fish   _____

7
mushrooms _____
muffins   _____
mulberries _____

8
peaches   _____
potatoes   _____
pasta   _____

9
spinach   _____
sponges   _____
spaghetti _____

10
syrup   _____
sugar   _____
soup   _____

Name _____

Unit 7: Alphabetical Order

Lee and Len are serving dinner in alphabetical order! Find the words in the box that complete each rhyme. The words must begin with the letter next to the rhyme. They also must be in alphabetical order in the rhyme.

a 1. Len serves the _____, orange and sweet.

Lee passes the _____, her favorite treat!

b 2. Next come baked _____ and soup made with cream.

And hot _____ from the oven—watch it steam!

c 3. Please pass the _____ that are so good to eat.

The crispy fried _____ just can't be beat!

c 4. Look! It's roasted pork _____ all golden brown.

The _____ on the cob is the finest in town!

p 5. A _____ makes a tasty pie.

The mashed _____ are piled a mile high!

s 6. The oysters and _____ are all fresh from the sea!

The salmon and _____ look great to Lee!

t 7. They serve _____ in a tossed salad, too.

After tuna and _____, they are almost through.

w 8. Now some _____ and berries with real whipped cream!

This _____ an alphabet dinner supreme!

carrots
turkey
shrimp
pineapple
chops
apricots
waffles
tomatoes
was
swordfish
bread
corn
asparagus
chicken
beans
potatoes

Ask your child to think of another food that begins with the same letter as a pair of words and put it in alphabetical order.

Unit 7: Alphabetical Order

Read each pair of guide words and the list of words that follow. Circle the words that belong on the dictionary page with the guide words.

RULE Guide words are the two words at the top of each dictionary page. They tell you what the first and last words on the page are. All the other words on the page are in alphabetical order between the two guide words.

1 money—narrow
moose
mask
nest
morning
name

2 stamp—stir
star
stone
sting
slope
steam

3 born—cattle
button
bold
cabin
brush
cave

4 imagine—join
inch
island
idea
jacket
journey

5 lamp—lettuce
load
laundry
listen
lantern
leaves

6 swell—tack
table
syrup
surf
straw
switch

7 double—dust
drip
dent
dye
dune
dove

8 entry—even
eye
equal
envelope
exact
escape

9 hint—hour
howl
honey
huge
history
hollow

10 burn—cable
bus
cone
bunk
butter
cabin

11 frown—garage
furniture
gate
flower
fuzz
gag

12 water—web
wave
wax
wander
wire
weave

Name _____

Unit 7: Dictionary Guide Words

Read each word in dark print and the guide words below it. Put a check (✓) next to the pair of guide words between which you would find the word.

1. creek
___ chance—clam
___ crab—crown
___ cheer—choice

2. boast
___ bark—beach
___ bat—bird
___ boa—boot

3. frost
___ farm—flew
___ from—fruit
___ frame—frank

4. leash
___ lamp—lesson
___ letter—little
___ leopard—level

5. pardon
___ pear—pilot
___ pant—people
___ pad—paint

6. saddle
___ sack—sail
___ sigh—skill
___ saw—scale

7. trace
___ tack—team
___ told—tonight
___ town—tube

8. either
___ dune—echo
___ effort—elbow
___ elves—enter

9. heavy
___ heat—heed
___ harm—haul
___ hem—high

10. imagine
___ idle—ignore
___ illness—intact
___ interest—invade

11. judge
___ jagged—jewel
___ jingle—jolt
___ journey—just

12. temper
___ teller—tender
___ tent—terrible
___ tenth—term

13. weight
___ week—welcome
___ waffle—water
___ waist—wall

14. allow
___ afloat—aisle
___ alley—almost
___ also—always

15. declare
___ damp—daze
___ depend—detail
___ deal—defend

AT HOME

Name a word. Ask your child to name two possible guide words for a dictionary page that contains the word.

188 Unit 7: Dictionary Guide Words

Circle the words that you can find in each part of a dictionary.

RULE Think of a dictionary as having three parts.
- The words in the **beginning** start with **A B C D E F G H**.
- The words in the **middle** start with **I J K L M N O P Q R**.
- The words at the **end** start with **S T U V W X Y Z**.

A B C D E F G H
I J K L M N O P Q R
S T U V W X Y Z

1 Beginning

beagle	lift	fussy	brave
mystery	honor	garage	kidney
decide	lime	candle	feast

2 Middle

large	quiz	plural	tangle
range	moment	native	kitchen
victory	outline	whistle	hinge

3 End

saddle	ticket	wait	rapid
unable	zero	trade	valley
probably	quilt	strong	x-ray

Read each word. Write **beginning, middle,** or **end** next to the word to tell which part of the dictionary you can find it in.

4. already _____   5. quick _____

6. rusty _____   7. hammer _____

8. water _____   9. basket _____

10. kangaroo _____   11. visitor _____

Name _____

Unit 7: Locating Words in a Dictionary

Read each word. Put a check (✓) next to the dictionary part in which you can find the word.

	Beginning: A–H	Middle: I–R	End: S–Z
1. event	___ beginning	___ middle	___ end
2. unwrap	___ beginning	___ middle	___ end
3. judge	___ beginning	___ middle	___ end
4. parrot	___ beginning	___ middle	___ end
5. sparrow	___ beginning	___ middle	___ end
6. finger	___ beginning	___ middle	___ end
7. desk	___ beginning	___ middle	___ end
8. igloo	___ beginning	___ middle	___ end
9. voice	___ beginning	___ middle	___ end
10. ocean	___ beginning	___ middle	___ end
11. certain	___ beginning	___ middle	___ end
12. insect	___ beginning	___ middle	___ end
13. whale	___ beginning	___ middle	___ end

Write three words that can be found in each part of a dictionary. Then number the words to put them in alphabetical order.

14. Beginning: A–H

_____

_____

_____

15. Middle: I–R

_____

_____

_____

16. End: S–Z

_____

_____

_____

Unit 7: Locating Words in a Dictionary

AT HOME

Name words and have your child tell the part of the dictionary in which the word can be found.

Read each sentence. Circle the meaning of the underlined word as it is used in the sentence.

RULE Some words have more than one meaning listed in the dictionary.

1. Write your name and the date on the test.

   date¹ the day, month, and year
   date² a sweet, dark fruit

2. First we will watch Dad use the camera.

   watch¹ an object that shows time
   watch² to look at

3. I will mix the batter until it is blended.

   batter¹ a liquid mixture used in cooking
   batter² the person who hits a baseball

4. This skirt and that shirt are a perfect match.

   match¹ things that go together well
   match² a thin piece of wood with a coated tip for lighting fires

5. This is a very lean piece of meat.

   lean¹ to rest against
   lean² without much fat

6. I put the box on the scale.

   scale¹ a weighing machine
   scale² in music, a series of tones

Write the letter for the sentence in which the underlined word has the same meaning as it does in the sentence in dark print.

___ 7. **Those books are mine.**
   a. The settlers found a gold mine.
   b. I know which fossil is mine.
   c. They mine copper in that state.

___ 8. **I will press the doorbell.**
   a. Don't press those computer keys too hard.
   b. The press sent reporters to the White House.
   c. I can press my own clothes.

___ 9. **The hero has the will to win.**
   a. I will go to the store now.
   b. The lawyer sent me a copy of my will.
   c. The patient has a strong will to live.

___ 10. **I gave the book back to Pam.**
   a. I hurt my back when I fell.
   b. Dan gave my pen back to me.
   c. Mom sat in the back of the room.

Name _____

Unit 7: Multiple-Meaning Words

Read each sentence and the definitions at the right. Write the number of the definition for the underlined word.

1. ___ Sam picked out a <u>present</u> for Jasmin at the store.

   present¹ a gift
   present² to be in a place

2. ___ Sam ran upstairs to hide the <u>box</u> in a closet.

   box¹ to hit with the hand
   box² a container

3. ___ Jasmin heard Sam come in and <u>left</u> what she was doing.

   left¹ a direction
   left² went away from

4. ___ Sam tried to close the closet door before Jasmin <u>saw</u> him.

   saw¹ a tool used to cut wood
   saw² the past tense of *see*

5. ___ Then Jasmin spotted the <u>tip</u> of the pink ribbon under the door.

   tip¹ the end
   tip² to turn over

6. ___ "Is that <u>mine</u>?" Jasmin asked.

   mine¹ belonging to me
   mine² a hole in the earth

Write the letters for the meanings that match each word.

7. bat ___ ___
8. can ___ ___
9. ring ___ ___
10. fly ___ ___

   a. a common insect
   b. to make a clear sound
   c. a wooden stick used to hit a ball
   d. to be able
   e. a flying mammal
   f. to move through the air
   g. a metal container
   h. a band worn on the finger

AT HOME Choose one of the word meanings above. Ask your child to use the word with that meaning in a sentence.

Write the synonym from the box that can replace each word in parentheses.

RULE Synonyms are words that have the same meaning or almost the same meaning, such as **strong** and **powerful**.

| arriving | autumn | breeze | collect | difficult | discover |
| entire | heavy | napping | storing | travel | types |

1. Dan and Wendy like to hike in the woods in the (fall) _ _ _ _ _ _.
2. They (gather) _ _ _ _ _ _ _ leaves and bring them back home.
3. In the woods they (find) _ _ _ _ _ _ _ _ nature.
4. Can you guess what (kinds) _ _ _ _ _ of animals they see?
5. They see a red fox (sleeping) _ _ _ _ _ _ _ in a cave.
6. A squirrel is (saving) _ _ _ _ _ _ _ nuts for the winter.
7. The hawk high in a tree is (hard) _ _ _ _ _ _ _ _ _ to see.
8. The caterpillar has grown a nice (thick) _ _ _ _ _ coat.
9. Some animals (move) _ _ _ _ _ _ to warmer places in the winter.
10. Others sleep through the (whole) _ _ _ _ _ _ winter.
11. The children know that winter is (coming) _ _ _ _ _ _ _ _ at home, too.
12. They smell smoke from the fireplace and feel the cool (wind) _ _ _ _ _ _.

Write the letters from the shaded boxes above. _ _ _ _ _ _

Unscramble the letters to find a synonym for **woods**. _ _ _ _ _ _

Name _____

Unit 7: Synonyms   193

Read each word in dark print. Then read the sentence. Find and circle the antonym for the word in dark print.

RULE Antonyms are words that have opposite meanings, such as **young** and **old**.

1. **early** — Aunt Sally arrived **late** to pick us up after school.
2. **remembered** — She **forgot** that we had to go to the dentist.
3. **evening** — Mom asked Aunt Sally to take us to the dentist this **morning**.
4. **distant** — Aunt Sally lives in a **nearby** town.
5. **long** — She drives the **short** distance to our house every week.
6. **before** — Aunt Sally took us to a restaurant **after** our checkups.
7. **ashamed** — She is **proud** of us because we take care of our teeth!
8. **light** — When we arrived at home, it was **dark** outside.

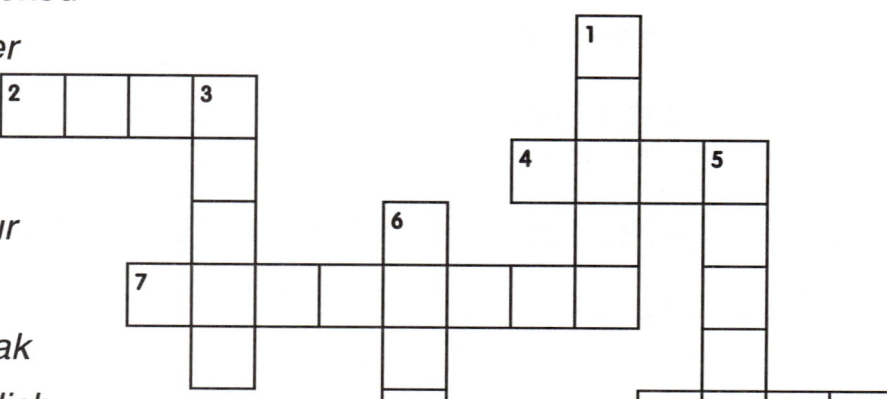

Read each clue. Use the words in the box to complete the puzzle.

Across
2. antonym for *polite*
4. antonym for *more*
7. antonym for *crooked*
8. antonym for *over*

Down
1. antonym for *sour*
3. antonym for *full*
5. antonym for *weak*
6. antonym for *foolish*

| empty | less | rude | straight |
| strong | sweet | wise | under |

Name a word and ask your child to give the antonym.

Unit 7: Antonyms

Read each pair of homonyms and their meanings. Write each homonym beside its meaning.

RULE Homonyms are words that sound the same but have different spellings and meanings, such as **hear** and **here**.

1. pair   pear

    _____ two matching items

    _____ a fruit

2. sense   cents

    _____ pennies

    _____ sight, smell, or taste

3. blue   blew

    _____ what the wind did

    _____ a color

4. road   rode

    _____ a street

    _____ took a ride

5. buy   by

    _____ near or close to

    _____ to pay money for

6. sighed   side

    _____ let out a deep breath

    _____ the right or left part

Circle the homonym that makes sense in each sentence. Write the word on the line.

7. A large _____ drank from the pond in our yard. deer / dear

8. I was very quiet so the deer would not _____ me. hear / here

9. I will _____ a letter to tell my grandpa about it. right / write

10. We saw _____ deer when Grandpa came to visit last month. one / won

11. He _____ a lot about deer. nose / knows

Name _____

Unit 7: Homonyms

195

Read each sentence and the homonyms in parentheses. Circle the homonym that belongs in the sentence. Then use the other homonym to write a sentence.

1. Our dog, Shelby, has long legs and large (pause, paws).

   _____

2. When she jumps, you can (see, sea) how big she really is.

   _____

3. Shelby is not a (week, weak) dog, either.

   _____

4. Even her (tale, tail) is bushy and strong.

   _____

5. We don't know (weather, whether) she'll grow much more.

   _____

6. Shelby walks (write, right) by my side when she is on her leash.

   _____

7. Last week the veterinarian (wade, weighed) Shelby.

   _____

8. I showed her how Shelby can (role, roll) over, too.

   _____

AT HOME Choose a homonym pair. Ask your child to spell both words and give their meanings.

Use the words in the box to complete the puzzle.

PHONICS and SPELLING

| difficult | easy | entire | present | right |
| throne | thrown | watch | whole | wrong |

Across
1. an antonym for *right*
3. an antonym for *easy*
4. a synonym for *entire*
5. a homonym for *thrown*
8. a word that means both "a gift" and "to be there"
9. a synonym for *tossed*

Down
1. a word that means both "a timepiece" and "to look at"
2. a homonym for *write*
6. a synonym for *simple*
7. a word that comes between *enemy* and *escape* in the dictionary

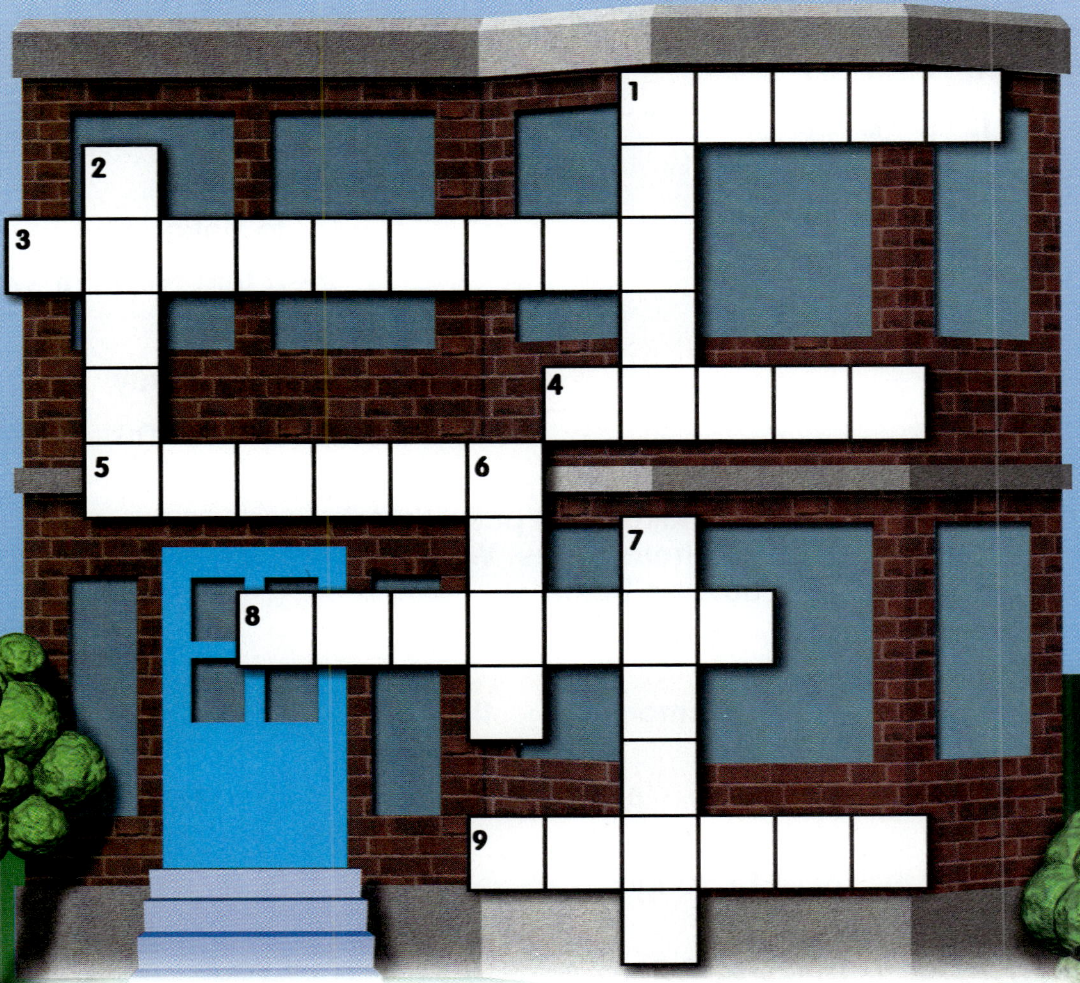

Name _____

Unit 7: Spelling Multiple-Meaning Words, Synonyms, Antonyms, and Homonyms

197

Circle the words that belong on the dictionary page with each pair of guide words.

1 **beech—best**	2 **garden—gift**	3 **mammal—meadow**	4 **rhyme—route**
before	gorge	matter	rose
box	gate	mantle	rhinoceros
beg	giant	majesty	rigid

Find and circle four words with multiple meanings in the puzzle. Write each word next to its definitions.

```
l  j  l  d  c  p  s
e  c  w  e  l  l  t
f  i  l  h  r  l  i
t  t  o  j  s  b  c
c  q  f  z  t  g  k
g  r  o  u  n  d  m
```

5. _____ — a hole dug for water / being healthy

6. _____ — soil, dirt / crushed into pieces

7. _____ — to poke / a thin piece of wood

8. _____ — went away / a direction

Use the words in the box to make word pairs that are synonyms, antonyms, or homonyms. Write each word in the correct column below.

| little | simple | smooth | there | thick | you're |

Synonyms   **Antonyms**   **Homonyms**

9. easy _____ 11. rough _____ 13. they're _____

10. small _____ 12. thin _____ 14. your _____

Unit 7: Dictionary Skills, Multiple-Meaning Words, Synonyms, Antonyms, and Homonyms Review

Point out words in a newspaper. Have your child name synonyms or antonyms for each.

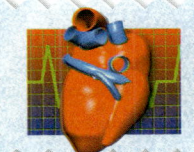

Read the passage and the poster. Then read the sentences at the bottom of the page. Write the word that completes each sentence.

PHONICS and READING

Safety at Home

Home is a place where you can work and play and feel safe. You probably don't worry much about safety in your house. But everyone needs to practice safety to prevent accidents. How can you be safe at home? Here are some safety tips.

Kitchen
- ✓ Put away all cooking tools after use so that small children cannot get them.
- ✓ Teach small children to stay away from a hot stove.
- ✓ Keep cleaning products tightly closed and out of reach of small children. Open bottles can be dangerous.
- ✓ Wash hands often, especially before eating and preparing food.

Bathroom
- ✓ Put a rubber mat in the tub or shower to avoid falls.
- ✓ Label medicine bottles and keep them on a high shelf.

Other Areas
- ✓ Keep toys and other objects out of walking paths.
- ✓ Keep long telephone cords off the floor.
- ✓ Put rubber backing on small rugs to prevent slipping.
- ✓ Check electrical cords for old or worn wires.

1. You can make your home _____ and prevent accidents.

2. It is important to wash your hands _____ preparing food.

3. Cleaning products should be kept tightly _____ and away from small children.

4. Keep medicine on a _____ shelf.

5. Keep toys _____ of walking paths.

Name _____

Unit 7: Reading Multiple-Meaning Words, Synonyms, Antonyms, and Homonyms in Context

Write a paragraph telling some things you can do to make your home safe. The pairs of synonyms, antonyms, and homonyms in the box may help you.

safe	unsafe
danger	safety
worn	old
eye	I
trip	fall
sick	healthy
hear	here
careful	careless
open	closed
listen	hear

Write the words in each box in alphabetical order.

1

arrive	_____
beware	_____
beneath	_____
allow	_____
alarm	_____
complete	_____
below	_____
concrete	_____

2

question	_____
prepare	_____
stream	_____
prove	_____
quiet	_____
pound	_____
strange	_____
pearl	_____

Read each sentence and the two definitions that follow. Put a check (✓) in front of the definition of the underlined word.

3. Mom <u>can</u> make the best cakes in the world.

  ____ to be able   ____ a metal container

4. She mixed the <u>batter</u> for my brother's birthday cake.

  ____ a liquid mixture   ____ someone who hits a baseball

5. It is a special cake made with raisins and <u>dates</u>.

  ____ the month, day, and year   ____ a sweet, dark fruit

6. Mom dropped the timer and now the bell won't <u>ring</u>.

  ____ to make a clear sound   ____ a band worn on the finger

7. Dad will <u>watch</u> the clock and take the cake out at the correct time.

  ____ an object that shows time   ____ to look at

8. Mom will wrap my brother's birthday <u>present</u>.

  ____ to be in a place   ____ a gift

Name _____

Unit 7 CHECK-UP

Read each pair of guide words. Fill in the circle next to the word that belongs on the dictionary page with the guide words.

1 journey—jump
- ○ juice
- ○ jeep
- ○ just

2 igloo—imitate
- ○ idea
- ○ ignore
- ○ injury

3 team—track
- ○ temper
- ○ trumpet
- ○ twinkle

4 drip—earn
- ○ drain
- ○ easy
- ○ eagle

5 west—wildlife
- ○ weather
- ○ window
- ○ wide

6 sand—scale
- ○ scrape
- ○ sailor
- ○ sauce

Read each pair of words. Fill in the circle next to **synonyms**, **antonyms**, or **homonyms** to tell how the words are related.

7 hour   our
- ○ synonyms
- ○ antonyms
- ○ homonyms

8 middle   center
- ○ synonyms
- ○ antonyms
- ○ homonyms

9 sick   healthy
- ○ synonyms
- ○ antonyms
- ○ homonyms

10 shout   whisper
- ○ synonyms
- ○ antonyms
- ○ homonyms

11 week   weak
- ○ synonyms
- ○ antonyms
- ○ homonyms

12 frown   smile
- ○ synonyms
- ○ antonyms
- ○ homonyms

13 large   huge
- ○ synonyms
- ○ antonyms
- ○ homonyms

14 journey   trip
- ○ synonyms
- ○ antonyms
- ○ homonyms

15 their   they're
- ○ synonyms
- ○ antonyms
- ○ homonyms

Unit 7: Assessing Dictionary Skills, Synonyms, Antonyms, and Homonyms

Circle the word that completes each sentence. Write the word on the line.

1. Have you ever had a bowl of _____ for breakfast?
      rice
      rise
      ride

2. I like green _____ and mashed potatoes.
      peak
      peace
      peas

3. Would you like some _____ juice on your fish?
      lemon
      lesson
      eleven

4. My favorite breakfast is _____ and eggs.
      hat
      ham
      had

5. We pick strawberries in _____.
      June
      Jane
      Jump

6. Sometimes I have melted cheese on _____.
      taste
      test
      toast

7. It is _____ to eat popcorn at the movies.
      fan
      fun
      fume

8. Mom will _____ a chocolate cake for my birthday.
      beg
      bake
      bait

9. Maybe she will _____ chocolate ice cream, too.
      got
      geese
      get

10. Have you ever eaten corn on the _____?
       cab
       cob
       cub

Name _____

Final Assessment of Consonants and Long and Short Vowels

Fill in the circle next to the word that completes each sentence. Write the word on the line.

1. Look at the _____ of snow falling outside.
   ○ lakes
   ○ flakes
   ○ snakes

2. Ana likes to ice _____ in the winter.
   ○ skate
   ○ slate
   ○ state

3. She and her brother _____ a cup of hot tea.
   ○ share
   ○ shape
   ○ cheap

4. Ana's winter cold makes her _____.
   ○ cough
   ○ couch
   ○ cuff

5. Winter _____ are long and cold.
   ○ knives
   ○ nines
   ○ nights

6. In the _____ Lori plants a garden.
   ○ spring
   ○ string
   ○ sling

7. Buds pop out on tree _____ in spring.
   ○ brasses
   ○ branches
   ○ brands

8. The grass turns _____ in the summer.
   ○ clean
   ○ gray
   ○ green

9. The boys camp in a _____ in the yard.
   ○ trail
   ○ test
   ○ tent

10. The _____ uses fresh peaches in summer.
    ○ fluff
    ○ chef
    ○ shell

Final Assessment of Consonant Blends, Consonant Digraphs, and Silent Consonants

Fill in the circle next to the word that completes each sentence. Write the word on the line.

1. The _____ travels from town to town.
   - ○ circus
   - ○ crust
   - ○ citrus

2. The workers visit many _____.
   - ○ candies
   - ○ corners
   - ○ countries

3. I like to _____ places they visit.
   - ○ studio
   - ○ study
   - ○ sturdy

4. I _____ for maps in the library.
   - ○ look
   - ○ lock
   - ○ loom

5. They set up the big tent _____ a mall.
   - ○ nick
   - ○ near
   - ○ year

6. Cold _____ can keep crowds away.
   - ○ wither
   - ○ washer
   - ○ weather

7. Sailors can tell directions by looking at _____.
   - ○ stairs
   - ○ stars
   - ○ scars

8. The group went on an ocean _____.
   - ○ voyage
   - ○ oyster
   - ○ volume

9. They took a _____ ship to Bermuda.
   - ○ crows
   - ○ cruise
   - ○ crawl

10. Tall _____ plants grew on the island.
    - ○ baboon
    - ○ bubble
    - ○ bamboo

Name _____

Final Assessment of *r*-Controlled Vowels, *y* as a Vowel, Vowel Digraphs, and Diphthongs

Circle the word that completes each sentence. Write the word on the line.

1. Carmen read the _____ scores in the newspaper.
   - baseboard
   - baseball
   - bathtub

2. The _____ played kickball on the playground.
   - childhood
   - childish
   - children

3. Ping _____ the ball the farthest.
   - kicked
   - kickes
   - kickked

4. Marcus jumped the _____ in the jumping contest.
   - highest
   - higher
   - high

5. Amy won the race at the _____ picnic.
   - familiar
   - family
   - famished

6. Every runner drank two _____ of water.
   - bottles
   - bottles'
   - bottle's

7. _____ going to play basketball at the park.
   - Where
   - Were
   - We're

8. We can play with my _____ ball.
   - brothers
   - brother's
   - brother

9. Golf is a sport I can play _____.
   - alone
   - open
   - aloud

10. You can go _____ in a lake or a pool.
    - swiming
    - swimming
    - swimmer

Final Assessment of Compound Words, Schwa, Inflectional Endings, Plurals, Contractions, and Possessives

Circle the word that completes each sentence. Write the word on the line.

1. On Monday the sun was shining _____.
   brightly
   brightness
   brighten

2. The sky was clear, blue, and _____.
   careless
   cloudy
   cloudless

3. Air _____ made Tuesday's sky look gray.
   polluter
   pollutable
   pollution

4. There was some _____ on Wednesday.
   impossible
   improvement
   proven

5. The _____ said that streets were flooding.
   reporter
   reportist
   reportable

6. I was _____ to find my umbrella.
   unable
   disable
   enable

7. It was _____ to stay warm and dry.
   impatient
   impossible
   possibly

8. I wished the weather report was _____.
   correctly
   correction
   incorrect

9. I was _____ that there was no snow.
   thankable
   thankful
   thankless

10. Friday was a _____ of the winter ahead.
    preview
    review
    viewable

Name _____

Final Assessment of Suffixes and Prefixes

Circle the word that matches each clue. Write the word on the line.

1. It means the same as *begin*. _____ end / start / before

2. It sounds the same as *wade*. _____ wait / weight / weighed

3. It is the opposite of *day*. _____ light / night / sunrise

4. It means the same as *curved*. _____ straight / bent / beaten

5. It means the same as *large*. _____ big / small / short

6. It is the opposite of *hello*. _____ greetings / good-bye / goodness

7. It sounds the same as *deer*. _____ doe / dear / peer

8. It is the opposite of *outside*. _____ inside / outdoors / invite

9. It sounds like *won*. _____ own / one / over

10. It is the opposite of *over*. _____ above / under / hover

Final Assessment of Synonyms, Antonyms, and Homonyms